DEEPEST RED

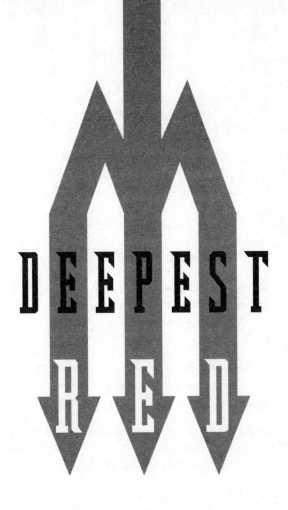

DEEPEST RED

A MANCHESTER UNITED ANTHOLOGY

Portnoy

PUBLISHING

First published in 2012 by Portnoy Publishing

1 - Limited Edition Hardback

ISBN: 978-1-909255-03-6

Printed and bound by: CPI Group (UK) Ltd, Croydon, CR0 4YY

Cover design: David Rudnick
Typeset in: Adobe Garamond by Sheer Design and Typesetting

Portnoy Publishing
PO Box 12093, Dublin 6, Ireland

www.portnoypublishing.com | Twitter: @portnoypub

LINE UP

ONE

MAGIC AND LOSS (AN INTRODUCTION)
BY BRIAN FOLEY

POOR SAMMY KUFFOUR. PROSTRATE on all fours, his sweat-glistened face etched with agony as he pounds the Camp Nou pitch with his fist. There is rage, yes, but also shock and sheer disbelief at what has just transpired. Nobody scores two goals in injury time to win the season's most important game. How the hell did that just happen? For Sammy, his teammates and for Bayern Munich fans hell would be the next few minutes, hours and days until, finally, they find redemption of sorts three years later when they lift the European Cup. For Manchester United fans the night represents a once-in-a-lifetime event. Winning the Champions League? Impressive, sure, but to do so while coming from behind as the match enters injury time… to win with such passion, verve and – bonjour Eric – élan. That, my friends, is The Manchester United Way.

So where were you 13 years later at approximately five minutes to six on Sunday 13 May 2012, when we found to our shock and horror that the spirit of Sammy Kuffour lives on within all Manchester United fans? So *that's* what it feels like to lose in the 94th minute of the season's biggest game.

The last minute of the last game of the season: it reads like a gypsy curse.

The pleasure and pain principle was at work that day in May. You can't have one without the other. What sort of pleasure is joy achieved without pain? You need the down before the rush of the up. We endure the pain of defeat so as to better savour the taste of victory.

Except, of course, we got that particular life equation somewhat back to front. All the victories we achieved over the past two decades and more came *before* the nightmare of Eastlands. The rollercoaster started at the top of the ride in Barcelona and from there it was a 13-year spiral downwards, with a few twists and turns along the way, before crashing at speed into the trough that was bloody Sunday in May 2012.

Seven months later I still haven't watched those final three minutes from Eastlands. Why would I? A few memories remain, however. One is hearing about all the City fans who left before the end of their game, in tears, convinced they had thrown the dream away. Then, when they heard the celebrations from inside the stadium, they pleaded to be allowed back in. For some reason, that gives me great comfort. Clowns and their bananas: the tragic comedy of it is hilarious.

I watched the match in a hotel bar in the West of Ireland. To say the football was a minority interest that day would be something of an understatement. There I was with the barman and a smattering of American tourists who had little understanding of the importance of this particular 'soccer' game. With little atmosphere and no hope, I watched. Nonetheless, my guts churned.

I say no hope, yet where there's life there's always some sort of hope. On the other hand that hope could kill you. All week we had mentally prepared ourselves for defeat; there was no way City would slip up against a QPR side already in the dispatch chute marked 'relegation'. We could probably beat Sunderland but that's as far as hope would carry us. I've no desire to recount what happened next, except to say that when Jon Mackie put QPR into a 61st minute lead, I leaped off my stool with a guttural roar that frightened the bejesus out of the Yanks. Imagine screaming in a library; it was something like that.

Anyway, having no wish to scare the tourists any further I retreated to my hotel bedroom, where I watched the final half-hour play out on my phone. Squinting at a tiny screen (well, for football at least) with a poor Internet connection, it would take 90 seconds to switch between the two games. A lot can happen in 90 seconds.

Maybe it's time to move on.

Time to look to the future while celebrating past glories: after all, following United is partly about understanding our heritage. There is a depth, weight and heft to Manchester United that defies crushing disappointments, like losing the title to City. Ask yourself, which club would you rather support? The one chasing its 20th title, or a club that has a page on its website welcoming new fans with: "We wear blue…"

So what of the future? If the changes of the past 20 years were a benchmark, then it would be foolish to attempt a prediction of what the next two decades might bring. We're up to our necks in debt, with owners who have no emotional attachment to the club. The Theatre of Dreams has long since lost its emotional punch, co-opted by the marketers with another slogan to sell.

On the face of it, we're not in great shape. City grow ever stronger, Fergie is coming close to the end of his phenomenal career, and we've ridden the crest of a wave for so long the odds of staying there diminish with every season. The new manager will have the unenviable task of replacing a legend. It has all the makings of an extended period in the doldrums.

In a way, though, does the future really matter? I mean, we the fans will still be here whatever the results. We're here for the long haul, even if that means Thursday nights on Channel Five.

Editing a book about Manchester United is a rare privilege, one where you read the club's history through the memories and experiences of others, from professional writers to lifelong United supporters. The writers you will find in this anthology come from a variety of backgrounds and generations, but the one thing they all share is a deep, abiding love for United. Whether it's the supporter writing about his first trip to OT in 1976, or the man who saw the Busby Babes play glorious football in the 1950s, to the guy who was *there* in '99, or the fellow who stood on the terraces when 'Ta ra Fergie' was unveiled ten years earlier, all have captured a brief moment of history. Each page is testament to the joy and pain of supporting Manchester United.

While putting this collection together I also realised the sheer amount of history this club carries. Perhaps it's understandable that the recent past takes precedence in this anthology – there are standalone chapters for Eric Cantona, Roy Keane and Ryan Giggs – but look at the players who are only mentioned in passing throughout the book; the players who could have merited *at least* a chapter each: Bobby Charlton, Bryan Robson, Denis Law, Paul McGrath, Norman Whiteside, George Best, Duncan Edwards – the list is endless.

These stories span United's history from before the Second World War to the modern era, from standing on the Stretford End to eating prawn sandwiches in the corporate suite (not that any of these writers ever did that!), from the pioneering Sir Matt Busby to the steely, determined Sir Alex Ferguson.

My time as a United supporter began somewhere in the middle of these two great managerial eras: 5 May 1979 to be precise. It's always sunny in the past and the last FA Cup Final of the 1970s was awash with early summer sunshine. The FA Cup was still glamorous and stopped all the clocks; the idea of moving it from a 3pm kick-off not so much absurd as simply unthinkable.

United in red, Arsenal in yellow. Yeah, I know what you're thinking: jumpers for goalposts. But that's the thing about football, and sport in general; it acts as a soothing balm against cynicism (even when all the evidence points to the fact that everyone – the players, agents, managers and owners – are the most cynical bunch of ne'er-do-wells you will ever meet).

The match is now a blur of fleeting memories and emotional twinges. I could go back and watch the highlights on YouTube and tell you I 'remember' the game, but it would be a lie. I remember the sensations, though: 2-0 down with five minutes left on the clock.

We watched the match in the middle of my friend Barry's eighth birthday party. The game was nearly over, the jig about to be up. I supported United, my Dad and Grandad supported them too; it was an easy decision for a young kid to make. It was hell. Every other kid in the room supported Arsenal; it took me a few more years of growing up to understand they were supporting the winner. It just so happened to be Arsenal on that Cup Final day.

I didn't change sides; I couldn't even if I'd wanted to. The comeback was outrageous, it dazzled and captivated me. Two goals in the last five minutes when everyone thought United were gone. I stood, thinking: *This is fucking brilliant.*

Cue Mr Alan Sunderland, perm, outstretched leg; dream breaker.

It didn't matter. I was hooked. A team dead and buried at 2-0 down had the guts and sheer chutzpah to fight on and never give up. Death or glory. From that day on United would be the only team for me. It was the comeback that did it, always the comeback.

The Manchester United Way.

Brian Foley is editor of *Deepest Red* and a journalist living in Dublin. His first trip to Old Trafford was for a match against Liverpool in October 1985. He still misses the old Stretford End.

TWO

"TA RA FERGIE!"

BY RICHARD KURT

AN AUTUMN DAY DURING the midwinter of Thatcherism, inside the most theatrically intimidating stadium in Britain. Edging gingerly onto the hallowed turf, dwarfed by the empty stands, comes a hesitant, even unprepossessing working-class Glaswegian; his blazer a bit too stiff, his tie too tied, his slacks not slack enough. Old Trafford is much bigger today than it used to be: it's now an unwieldy Leviathan, its sky-kissing top tiers endure their own separate weather systems, the whole actually too huge to take in with one glance, whatever your vantage point. But even in

1986, and even when deserted, OT could chill even the most arrogant ardour. And Mr Alex Ferguson was not yet the domineering, fearsome, cocksure knight of the football realm that he is today.

He turns towards the Main Stand, his back to the majestic cantilever, built by Louis Edwards with the money earned by Sir Matt's three great sides, and faces the nest of press reptiles gathered to mark the historic occasion. Later, someone would claim they had heard the circumspect Fergie repeatedly mutter under his breath "big club, this: big club". He himself would later confess to having felt the weight of expectation on his shoulders that day; he was no longer in Kansas – and certainly not in Aberdeen.

From the corner of his right eye, as he poses for pictures, he sees looming the great beast that has done for at least one of his recent predecessors; the sinister dark cave that cages thousands of what the 70s press call The Animals – the Stretford End. Here be dragons; here bay the hard core who ultimately determine the fates of those who dare parade hopefully before them – be they manager or player.

It takes a great deal to make a Manchester United fan of any stripe boo his own kind; it's been a badge of honour down the decades for Reds that we don't turn our backs on The Shirts in action. But as many a past rueful victim can attest, Old Trafford – and the Stretford End in particular – had its own equally effective way of making displeasure known. For example, players would sometimes talk of 'the growl', that unmistakable, frightening sound as thousands of unified United toughs tell you they are displeased. Whatever you did to invoke it, you certainly didn't want to do it again.

Old Trafford preferred, if possible, to keep its cast list in order, *not* by failing to turn up to games, or by booing, or trashing players' cars – these were the methods of yer Scousers, Bitters, Italians et al. No, OT would just give you the equivalent of a mobster's hard stare. No more need be said: you'd fallen short, and if you didn't want to fall into some concrete boots, you'd better shape up.

Dave Sexton, infamously, had failed to heed such warnings five years earlier; he would be sacked despite finishing the season with a seven-match winning streak. Winning is never enough at United: Martin Edwards, barely a year into the top job, would never again show as acute an understanding of fans' sentiment as he did that summer when he stunned the football world by unceremoniously sacking the man. Hardly a single supporter objected, to the mystification of many outsiders. But this is Old Trafford; it plays by its own rules and standards. Sexton had taken us into Europe, to a Cup Final, and to a last-day tilt at the Holy Grail league title – yet it counted for nothing in the end.

We hated his football: it contained no glory.

It wasn't United: he had to go.

This, then, was the audience Fergie had chosen to try and please. How aware was he of the lessons to be learned from the Sexton era? For much of the subsequent three and a half years we often had cause to suggest "not at all". Understandably, perhaps, Fergie seemed more concerned with the fate of his immediate predecessor, Ron Atkinson, and thereby gave every impression of proceeding on the basis that whatever Ron had done, he should do the opposite.

Not that this course of action was contrary to his nature at the time; there's a clear thread of continuity between the way he ran Aberdeen and the manner in which he handled United. The classic shorthand at the time was that Ron had been a Cavalier, whereas Fergie was a Roundhead. Time would eventually prove that Fergie had much more of the swashbuckling, gambling spirit in him than anyone could have imagined in 1986. But back then, the analogy fitted.

Ron Atkinson, however, was not as much of an open-and-shut case as Sexton had been. Atkinson continued to have his defenders after the axe came down in November 1986; he also continued to receive plaudits for his achievements, even from those who'd agreed he had to go in the end. Ron's teams, for most of his five years, played The United Way, and did so populated by the type of individuals we loved to see in Red. Simply bringing the legend Bryan Robson to the club will forever elicit thanks from my grateful generation, as will allowing Whiteside, Hughes and McGrath to flourish. And when you consider some of the signings, like the beautiful Muhren, thrilling Olsen or stirring Strachan; it's too easy to dismiss those years – as some young pups do today – simply because we failed to lift the one trophy Ron knew he'd need to secure in order to survive as manager.

Footballing epochs often end upon sudden, knife-edge decisions. It's facile to argue in retrospect, even with 20/20 hindsight, that Ron was inevitably destined for failure – although that's the argument often made. His supposed negligence when it came to building a youth system, coupled with his overly laissez-faire attitude to player discipline, are often said to have made long-term collapse unavoidable. But during the midwinter of 1985-86 – only 10 months away from the sack – Ron was on top, and had produced the most glorious football we'd seen since the arrival of Gordon Hill catalysed the 1975 Docherty Boys a decade earlier. Had the Hughes Affair (a protracted transfer saga involving the Welshman and Barcelona) not started to poison proceedings, or had Ron's usual golden touch not deserted him in the transfer market that summer, United could quite conceivably have been champions in 1986 and 1987. The utter discrediting of Marxian determinist analysis has shown that nothing is inevitable in world history, so why should it be so in football?

Fergie understood his immediate task, for it was the same one Ron had been given: win the League. Now that we are all fat and pampered, practically stuffed with titles, it's too easy to forget what a howling void we felt within during those days as we contemplated the embarrassing humiliation of approaching a 20th year without a championship. The new manager injected temperance into the club's booze culture, applied some hard-headed tactical rigour to a previously carefree playing style, and made a couple of excellent purchases in Bruce and Choccy – signings that were still paying out dividends well into the later glory years.

By May 1988, Fergie managed to drag a hastily rejigged yet still quasi-Atkinsonian side to runners-up spot in the League, just behind the perennial perch-sitters, Liverpool. On the face of it, this was a triumph of sorts. Not only had we set a then club record for the fewest defeats in a season, but Fergie had turned us into supposedly genuine title contenders, just 18 months since that League Cup disaster at The Dell had sounded Ron's death knell.

Historically, the position of 'potential champions' had been a dangerous one for any United manager to reach. Every single one of Fergie's four predecessors lost his job within a year of attaining that pre-summit peak. O'Farrell was five points clear on Christmas Day '71, and five days on the dole come Christmas Day '72. Docherty had flirted with the title in '76 (and did more than flirt with the physio's wife in '77). Sexton had been runner-up in '80, but was run out in '81. Atkinson's vertiginous plummet from top spot to black spot took 10 months.

Yet, within this moment of maximum opportunity and maximum danger, Fergie made one of his bravest decisions: he would rip it up and start again (a decision subsequently described as hard, then foolhardy, and, finally, foolish, when the following two years unfurled with often horrific content).

We now know he was right; some even knew it at the time, such as Bryan Robson, (captain of the very Old Guard whom Fergie was soon to target) who would admit that the '88 team "was not good enough to win the League". Martin Edwards, who might have blanched when Fergie informed him of his expensive intentions in June 1988, instead took it manfully on the chin and delivered them to the Board.

Fergie himself, clearly grown in confidence since those nervous first steps in front of an empty Stretford End, had no doubts: "This isn't just a job. This is a mission. We will get there, believe me. And when it happens, life will change for Liverpool, and for everybody else."

That humble, blazered newbie of 1986 who'd looked like the Man from the

Prudential was being transformed into the Man of Providence; this sense of mission would henceforth never desert him. Even with various nadirs to come – such as the night of the infamous Crystal Palace home defeat of 1989 – he remained unbowed, telling a doubting Darren Ferguson: "Don't worry. I'll win this League. It'll just take a little bit longer than I thought."

It would also involve taking a little bit more pain than he'd have thought. Over the next two seasons, there were grim post-defeat nights when – by his own admission – he hid his head under the pillow (and, truthfully, many a Red would've volunteered to hold that pillow down). There were days he was reluctant to leave the house lest he be accosted by furious fans, or taunting Bitters. "You feel you have to sneak round corners, like some kind of criminal," he groaned. And there were half-times and full-times of Hairdryer Hellfire, with Fergie bawling into the terrified faces of players, struggling to accommodate the ever-changing kaleidoscope their manager applied to selection and tactics. This was the era when 'Tinkerbell' first took up residence, that alter ego of Fergie's who, like Hyde to Jekyll, emerged at times of emotional stress to wreak havoc with bizarre formations, outrageous positional commands and baffling transfer targets.

The football wasn't actually much good during 1987-88, at least not by the standards United fans judge these things. But at least it produced results, dispelling any lingering fears which emerged the previous season, namely that United might be entering a period of relegation fighting (such as we'd been through in the early years of both the 60s and 70s). Yet, over the next two seasons, the football alarmingly worsened: results started souring. Now, United fans will put up with entertainment without trophies; they'll also put up with trophies without entertainment. But, as Mr Micawber might have put it, "no trophies plus no entertainment – result: misery."

Incredibly, the nightmare of scrapping to avoid relegation battles returned with a vengeance. You'd peek through your fingers at the league table in the Pink Final. Injuries were a factor, and many understood that this was a rebuilding period, one that demanded at least some patience. But most of Fergie's signings for 1988-89 were hugely disappointing, and beloved Stretford End legends, McGrath and Whiteside, were clearly en route for nasty exits.

Meanwhile, Fergie's great white hope on the wing was to be Ralphie

Milne, a player now totemic in modern United history for all the wrong reasons. "Is he supposed to be a winger?" I heard a Red ask during one of Ralphie's early car crash displays. "Is he even supposed to be a footballer?" came the mournful reply. A demotic phrase summed it up on the terraces: "This is beginning to take the piss."

J-stander Pete Molyneux was a classic home 'n' away Red. Working class,

local, loyal, time-served and passionate – but also bearing the justified sense of entitlement that comes with being 'A Proper Red'. That means you are entitled to say enough's enough when the moment comes, without having said Redness questioned.

Like all of us, he was still smarting from the 5-1 derby defeat, as perfect an expression of this era's wretchedness as you could conceive. At 4.05pm on the notorious afternoon of 9 December 1989, when a Crystal Palace side full of no-mark trundlers beat a spectacularly inept and Hughes-free United 2-1, Pete stood up on his seat and, with the help of five mates, unveiled a banner. It was fashioned from what is probably the most famous bed-sheet ever manufactured by old Cottonopolis, because what had been painted on it was so shockingly out of character for us, and so wryly regarded in retrospect:

'3 years of excuses and it's still crap...Ta ra Fergie!'

Ouch. And, umm, ouch again.

'Ta ra Fergie!' – it had a seasoned copywriter's genius to it, and Reds of a certain age will instantly know what you're talking about if you quote it to them. Pete explains it in his forthcoming memoirs: "I was considering finishing off with 'Fergie Out!' or 'Fergie Must Go!' but, being a Salford lad, *Coronation Street* came to mind. The superb Bet Lynch was at her peak as landlady of the Rovers Return Inn and her parting shot to all and sundry as they headed out was always an endearing "Ta ra, cock: goodnight!" Perfect. It had to be 'Ta ra Fergie!' "

Unquestionably, he spoke for many in the stadium, although debate would chunter on for months among

DEEPEST RED: A MANCHESTER UNITED ANTHOLOGY

ourselves as to whether he had been right to take the final step in, quite literally, displaying our dirty bed linen to the world. For example, I wasn't one of the 'Fergie Out' brigade myself – contrary to reputation, I never have been – but I remember arguing for Pete's right to express a widely held view on Voltairean principle. On the day, it was hard for many to resist at least applauding the lad's spirit, as Pete recalls: "I didn't know how the protest would be received; I couldn't recall a similar incident at Old Trafford in 26 years of watching United. The diehards on United Road noticed it first; their spontaneous reaction was loud cheering and applauding. Within seconds, cheers rippled around the ground like one of those long lines of falling dominoes. The ovation grew in volume as it travelled, reaching a deafening crescendo at the Stretford End."

Doubtless there'll be a few blushes from even redder Reds when they remember that day, especially if they were among the cheering hordes. But even Paddy Crerand, now famed for being the most blinkered of 'Fergie's United' zealots, had joined in some of the criticism of Fergie and his side, though not to the same extent as his old pal Georgie Best, who declared: "I wouldn't walk round the corner to watch this team play."

Yet, just six months later, we were walking all the way around the corner and down Wembley Way (twice) to watch this very same team play, triumph, and thereby kickstart the greatest golden era of any club in English history.

Again, it's all about knife-edge moments. Just as Ron might have become the one with a knighthood and OT empire had he played one or two better cards at the right moment, so too might Alex have joined Wilf, Frank and Dave in the 'also-rans' paddock. When substitute Mark Robins's effort crossed the line at the City Ground in January's third round FA Cup tie, he went down in imperishable history, forever labelled as 'The man who saved Fergie's job'.

Naturally, today, everyone involved insists – and, to be fair, insisted at the time (at least publicly) – that no such importance rode on that ball as it headed towards the net. Indeed, the moment has gone down in history for another reason: it inspired the standard line trotted out every time a manager is in trouble at a football club. "Remember Fergie in 1990," the wise-acres intone, reminding us how much United would have thrown away in future gold had they succumbed to the easy option and binned Fergie that New Year.

There are those who'll tell you that, despite all such protestations, Fergie was astride the knife edge that afternoon – in the most immediate, testicle-threatening fashion. United's coach driver on that day would later claim to the *Daily Mirror* that Martin Edwards, leaning over to cadge a crafty fag as they waited to set off for Nottingham, told him Fergie would be sacked if United lost that match.

Certainly, one is left to wonder what might have come to pass in the summer of 1990 had United not won the FA Cup in such a stirring, backs-to-the-wall fashion. Imagine if they had been knocked out by Forest, or perhaps by Hereford, who gave us a hairy enough battle in the fourth round? United did not play great football in the Cup run; we certainly rode our luck. With the good – and some great – players in the squad, properly knitted together and organised, we should really have battered every team we faced. But after all the trauma they had been through prior to January, it was too soon to expect such things; at this juncture, all we wanted to see was some fight and pride, some sign that hope might be placed in the future of this Fergie United. They certainly gave us that – and the fans responded, with some epic turn-outs and vocal displays along the way.

Speculating on what might have happened had we not succeeded is typical of the great 'what ifs?' beloved by the counterfactual historians, and we can really only deal with 'what is': United had a trophy, we were back in Europe, and Fergie, at the very least, had bought himself some more time. If pride and fight are restored, that's the foundation in place; now you can build something on it. The bed sheets could be put away, the season ticket renewal forms retrieved from the bin, and the Board could dust off the chequebook that summer with slightly more confidence. Denis Irwin, a canny purchase whose eternal quality would repay the fee tenfold, marked the start of a new Fergie era in the market, one in which the hits finally out-numbered the flops by a good five to one.

And what of the great beast, the Stretford End, that silent witness to Fergie's first day at school? Temporarily sated by silverware, it would be receiving a huge new infusion of vocal talent in 1990-91 from the newly-de-funct United Road paddock, thus ensuring two mem-orably effective final years on the moribund terraces. The beast would have little cause to growl ever again, except for the prospect of its own approaching demo-lition, and the sight of a petulant Neil Webb flouncing off the pitch in the spring of '92. For the Fergie era had finally begun in earnest, and Pete Molyneux couldn't be happier to have been proved so wrong.

"Looking back," he says, "obviously the darkest hour was just before dawn. I still sat with 7,000 Reds and cheered United home in that Cup tie at Forest, of course. Thank God Fergie didn't say 'Ta ra' too! Of course, my mates have revelled in reminding me that I was the prick that wanted to get rid of him, and the stick I get increases with each piece of silverware the great man picks up. As every year passes, it makes me look like the biggest twat since Dick Rowe turned down the Beatles. But I've never regretted the episode. I felt it was the right thing to do at the time. And if United were ever in such dire circumstances again, I'd do the same. United supporters have to protect their heritage."

Pete may have been wrong on the day, but he's still got what being a Red's all about dead right. Ta ra for now, cocks...

Richard Kurt is the author of eight books about United, a contributor to the *Red Issue* fanzine since 1992, and United correspondent of the *Irish Examiner* newspaper since 1999.

THREE

TWISTED BLOOD
BY ANDI THOMAS

A THEORY. WINGERS ARE, pound for pound, the most exciting footballers of the lot to watch. Yes, there are perhaps more cerebral pleasures in gazing at playmaking midfielders, or earthier joys that come from hardened centre-halves and spittle-flecked enforcers. And yes, strikers have the goals, those explosive moments that are the point of the whole exercise, while goalkeepers get their own gasps by stopping them. But wingers thrive on that sweetest of footballing sensations: humiliation.

Wingers beat their men, they twist their blood, they turn them inside out and then they leave them for dead; if the language feels worryingly violent at times, that's because it's a brutal business. When it comes to inflicting these punishments, plenty of perfectly decent wingers rely on straightforward pace, space, and getting a jump on the defender. Others use intricate sleight-of-foot and swerve-of-hip to discombobulate their opponents. But a few, a blessed few, have both, and then have everything else – a decent cross, some finishing ability, good cheekbones, tousled hair, and so on. Such was the young Ryan Giggs.

When I was young, being Welsh, a Manchester United fan, and already knowing deep down that the wing was where it was at, baby, I basically had no choice but to adopt Ryan Giggs as my favourite and my best. As a kid, professional football isn't really a vicarious thing that you watch and experience in the watching. Instead, it's on the one hand a lingering fact of fundamental identity that teaches you to learn about tribes and rivals and glory and jealousy and (occasionally) getting your head kicked in. On the other hand, it's what you play. And whenever I played, ignoring such tedious distractions as not being left-footed (for which I've never forgiven myself) and not being any good (which I came to terms with early on), I was Ryan Giggs.

The trouble with longevity in sport is that it becomes its own achievement. Play forever, and the fact of playing forever starts to overshadow all the other stuff. This is not to denigrate Giggs's achievement in extending his career as he has, which is remarkable, but to assert that it's not about how long you can keep going, but how high you can get, and how consistent you are. On top of that, when it comes to Giggs, his status is exacerbated because he's a one-club man, an instance of those rare and precious footballers who flourish and wane within the same walls.

United have had just two in their history, Bill Foulkes and Gary Neville, though Giggs and Paul Scholes seem certain to join them shortly. It would be nice to pretend that such single-minded devotion is always a story of destiny, of shared loyalty and love, but it would be a lie. Such a relationship relies more than anything on the player and club being of roughly equivalent standard for the entire length of the player's career. Had Manchester United not been good enough to win titles in the 90s, Giggs could have ended up elsewhere; had Giggs not been good enough, United could have sold him. In football, affection is generally contingent on mutual utility, and while there may be the occasional exception to that rule, I suspect very few of them involve Alex Ferguson.

As an aside, I've always been slightly troubled by the idea that the one-club man is the ultimate club servant. It implies that despite his 758 games, despite his being as Manchester Unitedy a man as ever Manchester Uniteded, despite his being the longest-serving Holy Trinitarian, Bobby Charlton is somehow less of a servant than Gary Neville because he spent a season at Preston North End and played a few games for Waterford. All because he didn't have a Sky Studio to slip into.

So, if we set aside the longevity, what are we to make of Giggs? At times, he was utterly magnificent, making ribbons of defences in appropriate fashion. Where some shrivelled on the European stage, he thrived, taking particular pleasure in unchaining Italian defences; it's no wonder that Internazionale's Massimo Moratti has coveted him for so long. Three games against Juventus in consecutive seasons – 96-97, 97-98, and then the Treble year – stand out. A personal favourite followed in 2000, when Giggs, in one of those moods where every pass seems to come off the outside of the boot or the heel, or while facing the other way, sparkled as United came from behind to overcome Gabriel Batistuta's Fiorentina.

But there's a lingering sense that perhaps these moments were, well, just that: too momentary. In his excellent and recommended book, *On The Road: A Journey Through A Season*, Daniel Harris writes:

"Judging [Giggs] by his own stratospheric standards, any honest evaluation of his career leaves you wondering why he hasn't been brilliant more often." Harris cites the examples of those around Giggs in the pantheon – Keane, Cantona, et al. – and points out that Giggs, in their company, can lack both consistency and intensity, a fact only semi-excused by the fundamentally peripheral and service-dependent nature of being a winger.

This is perfectly summed up by the moment that will, more than any other, define Giggs's place in football history: that deliriously demented game-winning slalom through Arsenal's defence in extra time of the 1999 FA Cup semi-final replay. You often hear Arsenal fans make the point that Giggs, having come on as a substitute, was fresher than the defenders he exploded, and they have something of a point. But, in between coming on and deciding to score one of the greatest goals in Manchester United history, he hadn't been playing well at all. As he said later: "I started poorly, giving the ball away the first three or four times I got it, generally having a bit of a nightmare. So, I decided that the next time I took possession I wasn't going to pass it, I was just going to dribble." The rest is glory and chest hair, screaming and the treble, but it's a great goal, not a great performance.

Giggs clearly doesn't lack for drive, or focus, or ambition, yet it certainly doesn't look to the outside observer that this manifests itself in the kind of relentless drive for perfection that characterised many of his colleagues, particularly Roy Keane. There's little fury. When the off-day comes around, he doesn't bubble or seethe; instead the shoulders slope, the hands meet hips, the head cocks, and the ball bobbles away. That he's one of the most superlatively talented players to pull on a United shirt is not in doubt, and nor is there any question that he's done some of the more sublime things it's been my privilege to see. What's missing, perhaps, is a small thing, but a thing nonetheless: failing to bend the game to your will can happen, but not always trying to? That never should.

Actually, that's not all that's missing. There is, at least for me, something else that nags, something slightly deeper. Although there's always somebody that will dispute anything, nobody disputes that Giggs's longevity is a remarkable achievement in its own right. But that longevity is predicated on self-denial: endless yoga stretches, no butter on his toast, no sports cars and, most importantly, no sprinting.

That, I think, is where the vague sense of incompleteness comes from. Giggs chose to endure, but by doing so, he curtailed himself. Having emerged as the avatar of the blood-twisting winger, he recognised that a life chasing chalk dust would be a short one, and full of pain. So, like a sensible professional, he adapted his gait, his training methods, his diet, his lifestyle, and his game, and stretched his career out and on.

But, well, *wingers.* Wingers are rock stars, and he was my rock star, and rock stars are supposed to vanish in a cloud of excess, self-immolated by their own inability to stop being themselves as intensely as possible. Giggs – for legal reasons, I should make clear this is an analogy – decided to kick the heroin, rein in the booze, settle down with a wife, and make acoustic albums exploring his folk influences. Sensible. Professional. And just a tiny bit disappointing.

When Giggs emerged, the inevitable flood of lazy comparisons led George Best to chuckle that: "One day they might even say that I was another Ryan Giggs." In hindsight, he couldn't have been more wrong. Where Best consumed his talent as greedily and recklessly as he did everything else around him, Giggs rationed his; where Best flamed hot and quick, Giggs dialled the temperature down. You can see this even off the pitch: Best's infidelities are hailed as those of an amorous buccaneer; Giggs's are squalid and disappointing.

As another aside, the pitch and clamour of the kvetching that followed the revelation of Giggs's adultery was a perfect illustration of that peculiar interest people seem to have in assuming that their own distaste is shared by the rest of the world. The alleged 'failure as a role model' sounded desperately hollow; kids, on the whole, pretend to be footballers in the playground, not behind the bike sheds. Mind you, as I trust is clear from the rest of this piece, I had nothing invested in Giggs-as-Mr-Nice-Guy anyway. The destruction of something you don't care about leaves you cold.

To be clear, I am not saying that Giggs should have demolished himself the way Best did; that suggestion would be both offensive and ignorant. My point is that Giggs belongs to my childhood, to a time when there was nothing more important than running as fast as possible down the side of a football pitch. A time when it was worth straining a hamstring, if you were twisting blood. When you didn't need to take care of yourself because you were going to live forever. In order to prolong his career, Giggs sacrificed the posters on my bedroom walls; to accept that would be to accept mortality and the inevitability of decline, decay and death, and even as I tack close to thirty, that's not something that I'm particularly keen to do. Better to cling to an asinine and precious notion that Giggs somehow sold me out. Better that than growing up.

Unfair, yes; illogical, perhaps; self-defeating, certainly. But that's where the one-club man thing comes in. These devoted, exclusive servants are too pure, as footballers, to teach you anything realistic about the world.

Summer of 2009: swathes of young United fans watched Cristiano Ronaldo strut his way to Madrid and learned a very hard lesson about love and loss. Then they got over it and emerged as better and more complete people. But with Giggs, there's never been that moment of severance; he's grown older, diminished, declined, reinvented himself, and is now declining once more, and yet not only are those of us that skinned our knees in his honour forced to cope with the fact that he's sold himself out, but we've had to live with it, support it, approve of it, and cheer it all the while.

I hope it's clear this is not motivated by any particular desire to make tasty hamburgers from a sacred cow. Giggs is, without question, one of the most important and, at times, most thrilling of the United players I've seen, responsible for more moments of unalloyed and life-affirming joy than anybody has any right to demand. On top of all that, his late-career reinvention is in its own way a genuinely fascinating and possibly unique footballing story: a man, robbed by circumstance of his greatest strength, having to adapt and evolve in order to retain relevance and utility in a world that has little time for passengers and little sympathy for the ageing.

But there's the rub. That first Giggs, the blithe spirit that Alex Ferguson watched chase scraps of paper across muddy Manchester fields, is gone. Gone, too, is the boy who gazed up at him unquestioningly, demanding nothing more than constant and chaotic enchantment. In their place, a grey-haired utility player watches from the bench, while an increasingly realistic impression of a grown-up sits behind a laptop and tries to think up fresh arrangements for weary words. That, perhaps, is the ultimate lesson of Giggs's long career, his one-club fealty, his compromises and coping: that life, and more importantly football, is a constant exercise in making do, and that sometimes, making do is OK.

Andi Thomas writes regularly for *SB Nation Soccer*, *ESPN*, *Football 365*, *The Score*, and elsewhere. Much of this is eventually archived at twistedblood.co.uk Tweets - @Twisted_Blood

FOUR

THE UNITED WAY
BY BERNARD NEVIN

(Author's note: readers may notice that this chapter refers neither to Matt Busby nor to Alex Ferguson by the title 'Sir'. This is because many of the events mentioned took place before they were awarded their knighthoods.)

IT IS THE VANITY of football fans to believe that the club they support is special. But it is a vanity generally tempered by realism. Much as a man who knows his wife would not have much luck pursuing a modelling career will be nonetheless devoted to her, a football fan may proudly think of his club as 'The Greatest'. By which he doesn't mean it's the most successful, or that its team plays the most scintillating football. He means it's his, and that's what matters most to him.

Some clubs are special, though, by any impartial measure. Not just their history or their fame but, above all, their aura proclaims it. Manchester United is one such club. It's commonly assumed of late that what makes United exceptional is the astonishing success brought about by Alex Ferguson in the last two decades. For all that his achievements are unrivalled in the English game, that isn't so. The fundamental character of United, as Ferguson himself is quick to acknowledge, was established during the tenure of Matt Busby.

Busby's achievement was not only to rebuild the club twice – in the first instance all but literally, after Old Trafford was reduced to rubble by German bombs in the Second World War; and again, as a force in football, following the Munich air disaster – it was to originate The United Way, the philosophy that would distinguish everything the club strove to accomplish.

The United Way has often been reduced, in hindsight and for convenience, to the simple formula of 'winning with style'. This is to misunderstand it. Winning with style was not the foundation, nor even the solitary goal, of The United Way, but the product of it. The United Way can't be expressed as a single idea, because it isn't one. Rather, it's a kind of code assembled from disparate elements, one which deserves to be considered both in its variety and as the sum of its parts.

For a start, 'winning with style' discounts the equally important question of how one doesn't win. "Winning isn't everything," Busby famously noted. "There should be no conceit in victory, and no despair in defeat." In his later volume of memoirs, *Soccer at the Top*, he wrote: "If anything is to be gained from football, it is to be gained by winning or losing with dignity. If there are nations whose people so lose themselves in their emotions as to encourage the thug and the cheat they can be educated only by example. And there is no better example to a thug than to be beaten by a clean fighter. The defeat embarrasses the thug's supporters as much as it does the thug."

It should be noted that this claim was made in reference to international football, ahead of the 1974 World Cup. But it does have to it something of a Victorian quality that must have struck an archaic note even then; an evocation of the Corinthian spirit, and an implicit comparison between what is presumed to be the inherently British virtue of fair play, and the dastardly machinations of dubious foreigners. Yet, there is quite another way of seeing it: not as a rebuke to those foreigners, but as a prompt to the home nations of where their own best interests lie.

At its heart is a premise that rings true for many United fans today, and will – for example – see them condemn rather than praise one of their own players if they believe he has dived to win a penalty. (As may his own teammates and manager, if in rather more measured terms.) It's the premise that winning without merit is no victory at all.

It would be naive to suggest that no United player ever tries to con the referee or damage an opponent. The game has changed since Busby's day – and even then, the manager's outwardly austere principles were not a prescription for being gentlemanly to a fault. Upright as he undoubtedly was, Busby was also a tough customer who scarcely lacked for ruthless cunning, and his teams were fashioned in his image. This is the same man who observed slyly of his midfield enforcer: "Nobby Stiles a dirty player? No, he's never hurt anyone. Mind you, he's frightened a few."

For all that, the mores which govern football today are much more cynical still, while the stakes are higher than ever. Yet, there's a certain reassurance in knowing that neither fans nor staff will blindly defend a United player who obviously tries to pull a fast one or conducts himself odiously on the pitch. There are few English clubs, and none among United's immediate rivals, in which this stance persists even residually.

The question of what one will do to win is much broader than that of cheating. It's part of the attitude that defines how one approaches every aspect of the game. If, as has often been suggested, Roy Keane was the embodiment of Alex Ferguson's approach to football, then the player who filled that role for Matt Busby – with tragic brevity – was Duncan Edwards. Not even George Best was quite as emblematic of Busby's outlook as this prodigious all-rounder, described by the manager as "a Colossus first among boys and then among men." Whether he picked it up from his boss, or whether it was an instinctive impulse the young lion shared with the old fox, Edwards would help define The United Way – not only by his actions as the greatest among the Busby Babes, but in words as well.

In his book *Tackle Soccer This Way*, intended as a guide for other young players and completed only days before the trip to Belgrade that claimed his life, Edwards wrote: "Whatever precautions you take, the time is going to come when you will lose. Now I am not one of those people who believe that it doesn't matter whether you win or lose. I believe the object in starting a game of football is to win it. All the same, defeats will come, and when they do accept them as quietly and philosophically as I hope you do your victories." As with Busby's own pronouncements, this advice feels at once old-fashioned, yet timeless. It has echoes of Kipling's ode to the stiff upper lip, *If: A Father's Advice to His Son*, in which the Empire's poet entreats a notional youth to treat "triumph and disaster... just the same". But that doesn't make it irrelevant today. Whatever else alters in the game, both victory and defeat will abide.

You might argue that Edwards's counsel seems most useful for those who are in the habit of winning, and expect to; that it was intended as much as a reminder to himself as guidance to lesser players in more fallible teams. Maybe so; but that only serves to underline the point –who, after all, is more in need of recalling humility in victory and stoicism in defeat than an habitual winner? Even the customarily understated Busby remarked of the side in which Edwards was the youthful star: "In all modesty, my summing up of 1955-86 and 1956-87 must be that no club in the country could live with Manchester United." In the lyrics of his celebrated 1956 Manchester United Calypso Edric Connor coined the phrase, 'Football taught by Matt Busby', which United fans invoke to this day as the essence of The United Way.

So what is, 'Football taught by Matt Busby'? Is it a tactical template? An overriding ethos? The unremitting instinct to attack, attack, attack, attack, attack? It would be overly romantic to insist upon the last. Busby once remarked wryly that his typical pre-match team talk was a very simple one: "Whenever possible, give the ball to George [Best]." But he gave very different instructions before the second leg of United's 1966 European Cup quarter-final against the then fearsome Benfica. With a narrow lead to protect from the first leg, he urged his wingers – to this day United's natural attacking outlet – to stay deep for the first part of the game, and his team to "keep it tight", quieten the crowd, and snuff out the threat of Europe's best footballer, Eusebio. Within 11 minutes, Best had scored twice and United were on their way to a 5-1 victory on the night.

One thing this shows is that Busby had bred a team, and players, who overrode even his own occasional caution. Compare this with United's 2008 Champions League semi-final first leg against a shakier Barcelona side than anyone has faced since. Despite fielding a strong attacking line-up, United played with grim defensiveness, scraping a goalless draw. United went on to lift the trophy, but many United fans still view that game with deep distaste, as a betrayal of

The United Way which tainted the eventual triumph. Others would dismiss that view as far from pragmatic or even, in a favourite insult aimed at those who would hold United to the highest standards, "spoiled". Busby's core tenet – that "Winning isn't everything," which he echoed in those remarks from *Soccer at the Top*: "I hope sincerely that a defensive-minded team does not win the World Cup, be it England, Scotland, Brazil or any other" – is not one universally adhered to by modern United fans.

As with any vague ideal, The United Way opens itself to endless interpretation. Perhaps that's why "winning with style" has become the commonplace, if unsatisfactory, shorthand for it. One might less succinctly but more aptly describe it as: "Playing with style, as a team, with bottle and brio; and believing that by doing so you will win, if not everything, then enough, and in the right manner." That may not be so catchy, but it just about does the trick so far as the actual football is concerned.

Yet it doesn't end there. The United Way encompasses the questions not just of what kind of football is played, in what spirit, and with what intent; it also covers the matter of who plays it. That is, who may be considered 'a United player', rather than merely a player who happens to have signed for United. "He's just not a United player," you'll hear Reds say of one who fails to meet their I-know-it-when-I-see it test.

With true United greats, there's usually consensus – even if it takes a while. Cristiano Ronaldo, for instance, is now recognised as perhaps the single most technically gifted footballer to play for the club in the Ferguson era. (As the man who in the 1960s came to personify The United Way remarked: "There have been a few players described as the new George Best over the years, but [Ronaldo] is the first time it's been a compliment to me.").

Yet Ronaldo was a divisive figure in his first years at the club. One faction had him down as a show pony, a diver, a Fancy Dan who couldn't deliver when it counts; another as a player who summed up everything watching United was supposed to be about. The second faction won the argument, as Ronaldo became not just a thrilling but a devastatingly effective forward, who had lumps kicked out of him up and down the land and was never scared to come back for more.

Due to his overweening narcissism, Ronaldo has been admitted to the hall of legends only somewhat grudgingly. The United Way prefers its heroes to be imperious (Cantona, Keane, Robson, Schmeichel), low-key (Scholes, Solskjaer, Charlton, Irwin), implacably single-minded at their given task (Buchan,

Valencia, Stiles) or mercurial (Best, Giggs, the cult favourite Gordon Hill – tricky wingers all, a breed with which United more than any other club is associated; perhaps its first true star, Billy Meredith, permanently altered the club's DNA.) Those who put themselves ahead of the team are seldom forgiven. Likewise those perceived to be soft, flaky, lazy or lacking in commitment.

Thus, The United Way has long straddled the divide that separates English football from what the English used to perceive as the continental type, demanding both the self-proclaimed English qualities of robustness, willingness, grit and effort, and the once suspect continental traits of flair, skill and ingenuity which Busby prized in his sides. This is only fitting for the team which took English club football's first steps into Europe against the will of the FA, and represented the English league there at what proved to be a terrible cost.

The Busby Babes exemplify another key element of The United Way: youth, and home-grown youth in particular. United's most glorious achievements – the back-to-back league titles of 1956 and 1957, the European Cup of 1968, and the treble of 1999 – involved teams built around talent schooled by the club itself. Trusting in the products of the youth system was an article of faith for Matt Busby. "If they are good enough, they are old enough," he declared. "If you don't put them in, you can't know what you've got." Alex Ferguson would echo both the sentiment and the deed when in 1996 he broke up the side that had brought United its first league titles in a quarter-century, and remodelled it around the group of youngsters who would be dubbed Fergie's Fledglings.

Latterly, this creed has proved a double-edged sword. As United transfer budgets have shrunk under the Glazer regime, while the overall quality produced by the youth system has fallen away, reliance on home-grown players has become a case of making a virtue out of necessity. While it would be unrealistic to expect so remarkable a crop as the class of '96 to arrive again anytime soon, the number of young United-bred players to distinguish themselves in the past decade has not been significantly higher than the number given extended runs in the side even when they clearly did not merit it. It's refreshing to watch a young player such as Danny Welbeck who has so clearly earned his chance; but one thing The United Way never prescribed was that the club could not spend serious money on established players to bolster positions for which the youth system hasn't provided. Busby didn't hesitate to use the financial power generated by United's support in this fashion. You can't, for instance, play The United Way without a first-class midfield; and no informed, impartial observer would claim United have had such a thing for some time.

If the list of United's "most glorious achievements" mentioned above looks incomplete, perhaps that's because of another often misunderstood concept intrinsically linked to The United Way: glory. The word is associated with the club both by its fans ("Glory, Glory Man United") and its many detractors. "Glory hunters" is the customary sneer aimed at United's broad fan base. No United fan who uses the term "glory" in its proper sense would bother denying it. There's no shame in being drawn to glory. Just as long as you don't confuse glory with trophies, which is what those critics invariably mean.

Before the silverware glut under Alex Ferguson, United already possessed huge allure in England and globally. The trophy haul up to that point was impressive enough, but United's record didn't eclipse that of other successful clubs.

Prior to the 1992-93 season, United had seven league titles – a figure Liverpool had reached in the mid-60s, and Arsenal over a decade earlier. United's seven FA Cups were matched by Tottenham Hotspur, while Liverpool and Arsenal had five apiece. Europe was another matter; but here again on the improbable path from Munich in 1958 to Wembley 10 years later, the 'what' was less significant than the 'how'.

Trophies alone didn't imbue United with romance, establish it among the world's most famous clubs, make it a favoured destination for players even in lean times, and gain for it a multitude of fans far beyond its home city. The United Way did that.

What is "the proper sense" of glory, then? It was beautifully defined, not by Busby or one of his Babes, but by the brother of one of them. Jackie Blanchflower survived the Munich disaster, but his career did not. His older brother Danny was a mainstay of the great early 60s Spurs side which, with the Babes out of the picture, showed how it could and should be done.

"The great fallacy," said Danny Blanchflower, "is that the game is first and last about winning. It is nothing of the kind. The game is about glory, it is about doing things in style and with a flourish, about going out and beating the other lot, not waiting for them to die of boredom." Spurs, to give them credit, have by and large stuck to this notion ever since, with the result that they are much better liked outside their own support than many more successful clubs. United, who pioneered that philosophy in the English game, have generally done the same – and filled their trophy cabinet while they were at it. Older United fans take some pride in their belief that in 1981 United sacked a manager –Dave Sexton – not because his results weren't up to scratch (he had just won seven games on the spin), but because his football was just too dull.

If one looks at the United sides with which, since the Glazer takeover, Alex Ferguson has attained such remarkable success, it is hard to avoid the uneasy conclusion that neither glory nor The United Way have figured greatly. After the sensational football that took United to the title in 2006-07, the tendency has been towards function over form, towards percentage play, towards controlling games rather than making the pulse race, towards making relatively scant resources go a very long way. Yet, the majority of United fans seem happy enough with the silverware; only a minority – and again, "spoiled" is the label so often attached to them – question the manner in which it was acquired.

Under such conditions, one must fear for The United Way. It can survive only if the fans demand it. If winning becomes the be-all and end-all, The United Way will vanish from the club's makeup, and there is no guarantee it will ever return. Should that happen, Manchester United will be just another club – albeit one of a group more honoured and more popular than most – whose fans' vanity is to believe that it is special.

Bernard Niven, better known as "Trop", pledged his allegiance to Manchester United in 1974, and became a regular contributor to *Red Issue* in 2005. He would like to point out that worse things happened to the club in each of those years. He has been known to write about matters other than football. He can be found on Twitter - @Trop_briefly

FIVE

YEAR ZERO: 1974
BY MICK HUME

"The past is a foreign country:
they do things differently there."

LP Hartley, *The Go-Between*

ON THE MONDAY MORNING of 29 April 1974, I, then
aged 14, wore a black armband to school. Even for
our old-fashioned grammar school, where we were not
allowed to wear white socks (bizarrely considered cool
and hard by teenage boys in 1974), this was unusually
formal.

Nobody had died. The homemade black armband (fashioned, fittingly enough, from an exhausted pair of football shorts) was there to mark the relegation of Manchester United Football Club to the Second Division of the English Football League, following their defeat by Manchester City at Old Trafford the preceding Saturday. It was a genuine expression of my adolescent pseudo-grief over this catastrophe. But it was also an ironic message to the piss-takers of the playground: laugh it up, do your worst, but I got there before you.

Little did I know, that black day was only the beginning of the trouble. Over the past few years we have often been told that United fans have gone through "all the emotions" as a big match or a season reaches its climax. I would suggest there is one emotional experience that more recent generations of Reds have fortunately never been through: humiliation, as an object of national derision.

We are not talking here about the odd day of ribbing after a heavy defeat. This is about being called "the biggest joke in football" for almost 20 years – the biggest club that could not win the biggest prizes. And it all began in April 1974, when United were relegated from the old First Division and went straight to the top of the laughing stock market.

It would prove a formative, bitter experience for Reds of my age, we who went through our secondary school careers as losers. It helps to explain why some among us will often seem a bit downbeat about United's prospects, always quick to assume that something is wrong, tempted in football terms at least to 'Always Look On the Shite Side of Life'. It is also why we were so elated when United finally won the title in 1993, why we worshipped Eric Cantona as the player who made it possible, got the Scouse monkey off our backs and put the past behind us.

It also helps explain why some of us have long been expecting the glory years to come to an abrupt end. And, at the same time, why we are pretty sanguine about the prospect, hardened in the knowledge that nothing in football could ever be as bad as that again. Six short years after being crowned European champions, United finished second bottom of the First Division. The nearest equivalent "disaster" more recently was that in 2005, six years after being crowned champions of Europe again, United were "relegated" out of the top two in the Premier League, finishing third. Oh, the horror, the horror (the genuine disaster that year, of course, was Liverpool fluking the Champions League.) If you want to understand the mentality of the later middle-aged

United man, look to April 1974 and the ordeal that shaped us.

Before we go further on this journey into the foreign country called the 1970s, I need to make a 21st century-style confession of an incurable addiction that has often made me a social pariah: My name is Mick, and I am a Surrey-based Manchester United fan. Born and raised in the suburban wasteland of New Haw, outside Woking, in that southern county, I have supported United for some 45 years. This, apparently, makes me a "Cockney Red" since, in the view of the rest of the football world, a Cockney is anybody born within the sound of the M25, not the Bow Bells (even though there were no motorways in Britain when I was born). In recent decades we "Cockney" Reds have often been labelled "glory-hunters". Fair enough, sticks and stones and all that. But if we *are* glory hunters, my generation had to hunt long and hard for any sign of it through the generally bleak years of the 70s and 80s.

It had all begun so well. I began supporting United in 1967, the year they won the old First Division title for the seventh time – and, little did we suspect, for the last time ever. That put United level on seven titles with Liverpool, who would win it another 11 times before we were champions again. The following season United became the first English club ever to win the European Cup. There were two basic reasons why that Surrey boy signed up as a Red: George Best's right foot, and the left one that went everywhere with it. My Georgie Best European Cup Winner's pennant stayed stuck to my bedroom wall until the day I left home. What riches might it be worth today? Maybe even enough to buy a ticket for a match at Old Trafford.

But why, people have asked time and again, didn't you support your local team? The best answer to that is probably "What's it got to do with you?" – nobody needs to feel defensive about the village idiot tendency among football supporters. But if we're among friends, I might explain that actually, we did. It's just that in the footballing boondocks of Surrey our local teams were all little non-league outfits.

In my first year at secondary school, when Best was having one of his last great spells at Old Trafford (at least until he went on a bender at Christmas) and United were top at New Year, I spent the 1971-72 season travelling around south-east England on the team bus to watch Addlestone Town FC (deceased) play in the Spartan League, listening to the United scores on my tinny transistor radio. In 1973 we went on the coach from my old man's local pub to

Wembley, to watch Walton and Hersham FC of the Isthmian League win the FA Amateur Cup. Later that year we saw Walton draw 0-0 in the proper FA Cup against Brian Clough's Brighton and Hove Albion, an afternoon which I recall involved a fair bit of running away from the south coast's finest skinheads. Walton won the replay at Brighton 4-0 in a match that kicked off at lunchtime because there was no power for midweek floodlights during the miners' work-to-rule of 1973. Later, Woking FC enjoyed some famous cup runs.

All good local club stuff, but not proper football. For that you needed to pick a First Division team from some faraway exotic town such as Liverpool, Leeds or Crystal Palace, and stick to it for life. For me there could only be one. It was just a pity that, having sworn allegiance to United at the age of seven as they won their seventh title, in the following quarter of a century they would go on to be crowned English champions exactly the same number of times as Woking, Walton & Hersham and Addlestone Town.

It might still be deemed sacrilege to suggest it, but part of the blame for the slump that led to relegation and mediocrity lies with the legend that was Sir Matt Busby. For most of his long United career, Busby was the master of renewal. Always looking to youth and the future, Sir Matt built top teams through three different generations. At the end, however, he became obsessed with the present, on winning the European Cup with the last great team he had assembled. When they did, 10 years after the Munich air disaster, it was like an end rather than a beginning for the manager and his mainstay, Bobby Charlton, who, like Busby, had almost died on that frozen runway.

In the few years that followed there were odd spells of success and cup semi-finals – including being robbed in the 1969 European Cup semi versus AC Milan, when the referee failed to spot that Denis Law's shot had crossed the line even more blatantly than Bestie's drinking. But an air of decline and decay hung over the place. Busby retired, then came back again, and cast a long shadow over the doomed managers that followed. The team became clogged with players who, in Best's words, were "not fit to wear the shirt".

At the end of the 1973 season, it was becoming clear that the glory years were over. Tommy Docherty had been appointed manager before Christmas 1972 with a target of avoiding relegation. He met it, just. United finished 18th out of 22 clubs. By the start of 1973-74 the triumvirate who ruled 60s' football had been broken up. Charlton had retired to become Preston North End manager, Law had returned to Manchester

City on a free transfer, and Best apparently had been replaced by a bearded, bloated impersonator of his former self. Just how inglorious the immediate future would be was about to become startlingly clear.

The 1973-74 season began, as it would go on, with a 3-0 defeat at Arsenal. By Boxing Day 1973, when Sheffield United became the latest visitors to be gifted the points at Old Trafford, half of the season's league fixtures had gone. Of those 21 matches, United had won only four, drawn six, and lost 11.

It is hard to convey how grim things were back then to those who now think United have had a bad season if it doesn't yield a couple of trophies. Often in 1973 we would have settled for a couple of goals. The Doc (who the fans generally liked) has since maintained that his attitude was, if we're going down, let's go down fighting, with some style. You could have fooled us. In that first half of the season, United failed to score in nine league matches, and managed five no-score draws. They scored a less-than-stylish total of 18 goals in 21 league games.

One infamous statistic sums up the state of affairs. At Christmas 1973, the club's joint top scorers in the league were George Best, Lou Macari, Brian Kidd, Sammy McIlroy – and the goalkeeper, Alex Stepney. They had the princely total of two goals each.

The unfestive atmosphere around Old Trafford at Christmas was a sporting reflection of the mood elsewhere in the country during an era of recession, oil crisis, class struggle at home and war in Northern Ireland. Even Slade's attempt to cheer up the nation with the first release of their seasonal anthem 'Merry Xmas Everybody' failed to lift the gloom. When the great Noddy Holder sang "Does your granny always tell you that the old ones are the best?", United fans, looking at our new team, could only respond that Granny was right. As for the line "Look to the future now, it's only just begun", we were afraid Noddy was right about that one, too.

In January 1974, Edward Heath's Tory government tried and failed to cope with the miners' dispute and the power shortage by imposing the Three-Day Week. Electricity to business was effectively rationed, television companies had to cease broadcasting by 10.30pm (no great loss some said), houses were plunged into darkness without notice. The lights were going out all over England. For young United fans, things looked darkest of all on the football front.

On New Year's Day a golden era had come to an end, when the legend that was George Best played what turned out to be his last-ever game for Manchester United – a 3-0 defeat at QPR. George had scored his final goal in a United shirt a fortnight before, at home to Coventry – and even then we had lost 3-2. When Docherty told Best that he was dropped for the 5 January FA Cup tie at home to Plymouth (after he missed another training session to exercise his drinking arm), it was the insult that broke the Belfast Boy's back. After that match, George later recalled, he sat in the empty stand, looked around Old Trafford, and knew it was all over. So did the rest of us, Georgie.

By now we were even suffering the indignity of seeing teeny-bopper fans of the Bay City Rollers wearing the tartan scarves that had become associated with United in the early 70s. This forced us to abandon our unofficial colours, or risk being thought of as Roller maniacs. Mind you, some might have wondered if that was less embarrassing than being a United fan. Of the first 11 league games after the New Year in 1974, the Reds won one, drew four and lost six. They were not conceding many goals – only 13 in those 11 matches, thanks largely to the defensive rock of Aberdeen granite, Martin Buchan – but just could not score if they were in a brothel with Bestie. They managed a miserable total of five goals in that run from January to late March. The unthinkable – relegation – seemed inevitable.

True, there was a short-lived flowering of hope as spring arrived. United went on an unexpected run of four wins and two draws, managing 13 goals in those six games – more than a third of their total for the entire 42-match league season. Three of those decent results were secured thanks to four goals scored by Jim McCalliog, the only First Division goals he ever scored for us. McCalliog's brief twinkle as a United star was fairly typical of the team in those days. Docherty later flogged him off to Southampton, where Jim was to repay the debt by setting up Bobby Stokes to score the winner against United in the 1976 FA Cup Final.

But in any case, it was all too little, much too late. The run came to a halt with a 1-0 defeat at Everton. Now, there were only two games remaining. Even winning them both was unlikely to keep United up, but losing either meant sudden death. And the fates of the fixture list had decreed, no doubt laughing in our faces as they did it, that the first of those games should be at home to Manchester City.

City, too, were well past their best by then, stuck in the bottom half of the First Division table. But they were still too good for us. There were officially 57,000 inside Old Trafford, most of them standing, the second highest gate of the season. As everybody knows, it ended in the way a cheesy scriptwriter might have imagined, with Denis Law – the pre-Cantona King of Old Trafford – back- heeling the late winner for City. He was immediately substituted, looking as if he might drown himself in the team bath. I say ended, but of course that infamous match has still not ended today – it was abandoned with five minutes to play when United fans invaded the pitch after Law's goal, with the FA ruling the result would stand.

If you want to see the authentic style of the 70s fan, look at the hair, clothes and scarves in the pictures of that pitch invasion – far removed from all these 70s-set dramas today. Note also how affectionately those Reds treated the departing Denis, City shirt or no. Little wonder that when Law released his autobiography last year, and was asked on TV how he felt about scoring that goal in 1974, Denis the Red simply replied: "Next question".

So, United were down, and would have been even if they had beaten City. The last rites were performed on the evening of my Black (armband) Monday, when the final match of the season ended in yet another defeat, 1-0 at Stoke. Bad as things felt down in Surrey, we were of course fortunate not to be in Manchester that week – at least there were no City fans to rub our faces in it. Just as I was angry but glad to be down in

London in May 2012, when City nicked the title in Manchester with the last kick of the season. Sometimes there are advantages to being a "Cockney" Red.

The 1973-74 season proved again, as the wise Jimmy "Greavsie" Greaves used to say, that ours is indeed a funny old game, and nothing is forever in football. The biggest and most famous club in England relegated. It felt like Year Zero. The following season United cut a swathe through the Second Division – and the Red Army wreaked havoc from Cardiff to Norwich, apparently determined to show that we still had top-drawer hooligans. But while United went straight back up in 1975, it would be another 18 years of humiliation and Scouse domination before the club became champions of England again.

For the past 20 seasons, of course, it has been hard for many – especially younger – United fans to imagine that the latest golden era could ever come to an end. It is certainly hard to see how United could ever be relegated again. However, the dark days of 1974 are worth recalling as a warning that things can change – in more ways than one. After all, while the Reds were relegated, the team being crowned undisputed champions of England, who drew the only 60,000-crowd to Old Trafford that season, was a little-known outfit called… Leeds United. Whatever happened to them?

Mick Hume lives in London and had a season ticket at Old Trafford from 1993 to 2010, watching United win 10 titles. He is editor-at-large of Spiked (spiked-online.com) and writes the View from the Smoke column in *Red Issue*. He is the author of *There is No Such Thing As a Free Press ... and we need one more than ever.*

"COME BACK WHEN YOU'VE WON 18..."
BY DORON SOLOMAN

SOMETIMES THE BEST OF enemies are more alike than they realise. Aside from being geographically close with similar social backgrounds, Manchester and Liverpool boast football clubs that share a common ground. The mix of success, tragedy and excitement; iconic people, moments and places make Manchester United and Liverpool unnervingly similar.

At the start of my lifetime, only one of these clubs could brag about regular success though. Not that I fully understood why or how, but Liverpool had achieved everything my club sought to do. I'd argue

that I'm part of a fortunate generation – I only con-
sciously started to understand and love football at a
time that coincided with success at United.

Alex Ferguson has always believed – and preached
– that the only way to follow up trophy success is
with more success. As one campaign ends, he's already
building towards the next. This rightly would never
have crossed the minds of Liverpool fans in January
1994; they were comfortably the most successful team
in England, historically at least, and despite enduring
a pretty mediocre campaign to date, many of their
fans still felt the team would deliver success soon.
A near-four-year league title drought couldn't go on
much longer.

To be specific, it was the fourth evening of the new
year and a full house at Anfield welcomed the reigning
champions as their visitors. For an entire generation
of Liverpool fans the possibility that their most bitter
rivals could ever match their record number of title wins
seemed far-fetched. The very notion of it was abhor-
rent. As it was the first time the teams had met that
season, it meant that some degree of goading beyond
the norm was necessary. Bragging rights had shifted and
dominance, certainly off the pitch, needed reasserting.

The game itself was memorable and one that United
should have won. Bruce, Giggs and Irwin gave United

a seemingly unassailable lead but, as they often seem to do at home, Liverpool came back, scoring twice before half-time and finally grabbing an equaliser in the second half. The match, however, went down in United fan folklore for something that happened off the pitch. The Sky TV cameras picked up on a banner that had been unfurled over a stand. The message was clear:

"AU REVOIR CANTONA AND MAN UNITED…
COME BACK WHEN YOU'VE WON 18!"

As a wind-up it appeared to be a safe one. United may have been the better team at the time, but Liverpool had both history and a culture of success on their side. Their feat of 11 league titles in just 18 years during the 70s and 80s seemed destined to not be repeated. There was real money in football thanks to TV deals; many clubs were starting to bring in talented foreign players. The championship would surely be shared around and Liverpool's title tally count wouldn't remain 18 for long.

The challenge the banner laid down was notably aimed at Eric Cantona first, and then United. Not that it represented all Liverpool fans, but it seemed there was a subconscious appreciation and understanding of the importance that Cantona played. They may have soon had the Spice Boys, but we had King Eric and he completed us. Beyond the layers of hatred and rivalry, Liverpool fans both knew and feared that.

As the story goes, United would go on to win the title again that season as the gap between the two clubs widened. From then on, Liverpool would be successful in every competition except the league. It's hard to fathom why they rarely managed to challenge for the title since United's success began, but maybe they rarely held a team together long enough for it to gel for longer than just a season. That, or the fact they've only had quality in a few areas of the team rather than throughout.

By contrast, United have maintained a challenge almost every year, building on one title with another. Ferguson has provided a blueprint in terms of how to maintain success. Every time he's won something he's strengthened his team in one or two positions keeping the competition healthy and the quality high. The result has been numerous title successes built around a strong core squad.

Bizarrely, Rafa Benitez's one "fachts" season aside, the rivalry has become almost stale. Pre-Premier League era, Liverpool just about edged the head-to-head stats between the teams. Since winning that first title under Ferguson, however, United have been dominant, winning more than half of the league games and having a winning record at Anfield. While games between the two sides have remained intense, the modern day rivalry is more often than not defined by success and therefore Arsenal, Chelsea and Man City, in that order, have in many ways become more of a concern.

What was suggested by the banner that day was so unlikely, so staggeringly impossible to dare think, that subsequently it became part of United lore among the fans. Much like the Man City trophy ticker that hung on the Stretford End, the Liverpool banner became measurable. It didn't just make a statement, it offered a figure and created a target that allowed it to be broken. More to the point, the lifespan of a footballer meant that Eric stood no chance of literally returning should United ever reach such a lofty target. But the lifespan of a fan is considerably longer. While the players and manager come and go, the fans remain.

This was never meant to happen – United would maybe one day catch up with Liverpool, but not for a long time and probably not before Liverpool had only further raised the target number. The somewhat remarkable thing about the process of chasing down, catching up and overtaking Liverpool's haul of 18 titles is that some of the personnel contracted to the club are the same, even today, nearly 18 years later. The core group of supporters is of a similar generation too.

That triumphant afternoon at Ewood Park, where title number 19 was secured, was magical. It was an uneasy day – United played within themselves, but scraped a draw, earning the point they needed for the title with a game to spare. In truth, it all felt a bit subdued inside the ground, or at least it wasn't quite as boisterous as I'd imagined it would be. Maybe that was because United had seen out the last spell of the game by simply passing the ball around the defence, and Blackburn were happy not to challenge, as they were now guaranteed to stay up. What I do remember though is seeing the number '19' everywhere and then, only having left the ground, did it all really come together.

Every fan at Blackburn Station seemed to be a Red. On the platform and the trains songs were being sung, all were – in one way or another – worded to remind passers-by that this was a record-breaking title for United. Banners were being held up, often containing the word 'Liverpool' although the specific wording eludes me. Many hours later, as my train pulled into Euston Station, I got onto the concourse and even there was greeted by inebriated fans shouting about 19 titles.

That's the thing about rivals: when the two clubs are on a par, everything becomes a bit more intense. Putting aside the pride that comes with being the best club in a region, when there's the potential that the result can impact on silverware for both clubs, it becomes more personal and vicious. A new nervousness forms that's matched only by relief when things go well. This time the result, despite its unquestionable importance, and the performance were strangely secondary. United had drawn and played badly, but it was all about overtaking Liverpool as England's most successful domestic club side.

Most titles United have won have been about the success over the duration of a campaign and seeing off a rival, but the last two have had a much deeper importance. Winning them has been a fabulous feeling but achieving the unthinkable over such a short period of time, with Ferguson still at the helm, has made it sweeter. Title 19 was won with Liverpool finishing 22 points behind United and without European qualification. The mighty had fallen and would slip even further away over the following season.

In many ways, the roles between the clubs have reversed. It's not quite 26 years since Liverpool last won the league but they're as far off the pace now as they have ever been during Ferguson's reign at United. It's not that they've become irrelevant but, simply put, Liverpool are not a concern in the way they used to be. A great rivalry remains. It always will, but they trade on past glories and the historical nature of it. The fixtures are always intense, but Liverpool no longer trouble the upper echelons of the Premier League.

I've no doubt that the 19th title would have been celebrated wildly regardless, but the "COME BACK WHEN YOU'VE WON 18" banner has given joy to a generation of taunted United fans. The Liverpool fans who cockily displayed it are probably still around today, scarcely believing that so much changed in such a relatively short period of time.

Arguably, our enemies are going to need something to happen to rejuvenate the rivalry again – from a footballing point of view anyway. Some fans would love to see Liverpool drop off further, but a closely fought title battle would be just as exciting. After two decades of dominance, Liverpool were caught and overturned. Hopefully, for United, the same doesn't happen, and no banners tempting fate are made: there's only room for one club on *this* lofty perch.

Doron Soloman enjoys youth football, stats, tactics and cynicism. He blogs on Stretford-End.com and rambles on *The Huffington Post*. He also spends way too much time on Twitter - @DoronSalomon

SEVEN

"THE FUTURE IS WITH THE YOUNG"

BY BEN HIBBS

ON 16 AUGUST 1939, Manchester United held its annual meeting of shareholders at Old Trafford. The nation's gaze might have been cast nervously towards the continent and the menacing encroachments of Hitler's army but, for the time being, Manchester United's focus was on an ambitious sporting future. The 1938-39 campaign was a tough slog for survival in Division One, having only just returned to the top flight. Back then, that was typical United. Between 1930 and 1939 the Reds spent six of nine seasons in Division Two and although promotion was twice achieved, once as Division Two winners, the three top-flight campaigns were all battles (two of them unsuccessful) against Division One demotion. It's about as far removed from the modern Manchester United as can be envisaged. But things were about to change, and today's football club of world renown was beginning to definitively take shape

At the shareholder meeting, chairman James W Gibson presented the club's vision, setting out a blueprint that would ultimately be responsible for revolutionising Manchester United. Gibson began his yearly review by congratulating the first team on maintaining its status in England's top division and promised shareholders "a spectacular effort" to improve on 14th place in a 22-team league. But there was an undercurrent of wider significance running through Old Trafford. Gibson stated that while the club would pay the price required for players who would expressly enhance the first team, "we have no intention of buying any more mediocrities". Here's why: while the first team won Division Two promotion in 1938 and achieved a semblance of top-flight stability the following year, United's Reserves were winning the Central League, the A team (a collection of 16 to 18-year-olds) clinched the Manchester League, and Mujacs (the pre-eminent Manchester

United Junior Athletic Club, comprising school-leavers of exceptional talent) won the Chorlton Amateur League.

Gibson, a wealthy businessman made good through manufacturing military and work uniforms, was born in Salford and raised in Manchester and renowned for his staunch passion for the city. He had already saved United from financial ruin in the early 1930s when the club was threatened with extinction. Now, he was pointing out that, despite Manchester City's status as the city's top team, "there is room for two clubs in Manchester". Gibson's vision was shared, among others, by club secretary Walter Crickmer and Louis Rocca – a visionary figure who suggested the name Manchester United back in 1902 and who had performed almost every job at the club from tea boy to assistant manager. He then helped craft a pyramid of youth development teams and a scouting system. On 17 August, *The Manchester Guardian* ran the headline: "Manchester men for United", adding that "a Manchester United composed of Manchester players" is the club's ultimate aim. The new season heralded a new dawn, but just three matches in and the onset of the Second World War halted professional football. However, the groundwork had already been laid for a brighter United future.

It was the arrival of 35-year-old Matt Busby in 1945 that really brought United's plans to life. Busby had reportedly rejected an offer to become assistant manager at Liverpool – where he had spent time as a player – because of various differences. At Old Trafford he had no such obstructions. Well, except that the stadium lay in ruins after a German bombing raid in 1941. Busby insisted on a five-year contract, such were his long-term intentions and devotion to the project. In this era of post-war struggle and reconstruction, Busby's vision was to build a club, a family club, from top to bottom.

His ideals aligned perfectly with the pre-War proposition set out by Gibson, and within three years United triumphed in the FA Cup in 1948. As if honouring Gibson's plans, the first of Busby's three great United sides during 25 years in charge at Old Trafford boasted six youth players: Johnny Carey, John Aston Snr, Charlie Mitten, Stan Pearson, John Anderson and Johnny Morris. Even the likes of Jack Rowley, signed for £3,000 from Bournemouth, joined two weeks after turning 17 in October 1937 – again a nod to the new-found devotion to finding talented youngsters

United's post-war transformation could barely have contrasted more brightly with the murky gloom of the

1930s. The pre-war youth players were, by now, grown men. Busby's managerial mastery was in team-building; he altered the positions of several players and formed the 'Famous Five' forwards of Delaney, Pearson, Rowley, Morris and Mitten. However, although immediate first team success was important, the club's new philosophy ran deeper than the 11 men on the pitch on a Saturday. The challenge was not to build one team, but a constantly evolving one.

In that sense, Busby's first, and most important, signing in 1945 was Jimmy Murphy, whom he appointed assistant manager. Murphy's remit was much broader than such a title commands today. His chief role was to develop players in the Reserves and Youth sides. Before the War, Busby, then a player with Manchester City, had played against Murphy at West Bromwich Albion, but it was during a chance encounter in Bari, Italy – Busby was managing an army team and Murphy was in charge of a sports recreation centre – that their partnership was cemented. Murphy was coaching players and Busby, who had already been offered the job at United, watched with interest. He quickly realised that, in Murphy, he had found "the man who will help create a pattern that runs through several teams of players, from fifteen years of age upwards to the first team".

Many players, Bobby Charlton among them, cite Murphy as absolutely central to their development. This, in essence, was Busby's talent: with a broader aim in mind he found the right people to do the best job. Murphy was integral to United's youthful revolution. The aim was a threefold commitment: identify the best young players – not just from Manchester, but throughout Britain and Ireland; develop their talent; and, finally, with the maxim "if you're good enough, you're old enough" give the players a chance in the first team. That model may have been adapted and advanced, but its basic principles are prized by Sir Alex Ferguson and United's expansive Academy.

Murphy was involved in the talent-spotting, but chief scout Joe Armstrong led the search with half a dozen scouts and various contacts within schools and youth clubs to ensure that United attracted the country's best boys. Once the players had signed, the transition from potential to first team success was unprecedented. Busby's early United teams weren't regarded as overtly flamboyant. Neither did they have, say, the distinctive long-ball style of Wolverhampton Wanderers – one of United's great rivals in the 1950s when it came to producing young players. Murphy drummed into his young charges the importance of crisp, accurate passing, to play simple but effective football, and to be able to adapt to a variety of opposition styles. The United youths of the 50s cut their teeth playing in 'open age' leagues across Manchester against teams that could contain dockers or factory workers. Wily wisdom was imperative to survival. Players talked of crunching tackles, sly digs and a raging desire to beat United, so the young lads had to use all their natural ability and technical training to overcome brute strength, and lots of it.

The youth players typically signed amateur contracts on leaving school at the age of 15, and were placed in digs near Old Trafford. They were also given the option of staying on at school, getting a job, or working on the groundstaff, which meant doing odd jobs at Old Trafford such as painting the stadium or sweeping up the terraces. Bill Foulkes was as tough as old football boots and worked down the pits at St Helens before turning up for youth team training on Tuesday and Thursday evenings. During training, Murphy and his assistant Bert Whalley who, tragically, was among the 23 to lose their lives in Munich, had their young players practising 'shadow play' – in-game manoeuvres, without any opposition, enacting specific passages of play expected during games. But everything was done with a ball and technique was crucial. Physical fitness was gained through playing.

Murphy – who lived and breathed football, and United – was attentive, too, offering regular one-to-one sessions for players to discuss their game. This returns to the notion of being part of a family club. Busby and Murphy were seen as paternal figures to the players, who were all properly looked after while on club duty. Vitally, the players all grew up together. They socialised together, trained and played together. Dennis Viollet, one of the original Busby Babes and one of United's finest home-grown finishers, said once: "We were like brothers, not pals." The club's sense of family always prevailed. To a large degree, it still does.

The hard work behind the scenes paid dividends on the field. The FA Youth Cup was introduced for the 1952-53 season and United won the trophy for the first five years in a row. It wasn't just United's first team making pioneering ventures into European football; in 1954, the youth team embarked on a first trip to Zurich, Switzerland, for the prestigious Blue Stars tournament. As well as the camaraderie and cultural education of trips overseas, the players were being prepared again for something bigger: not just domestic dominance, but European eminence.

United's first team won league titles in 1952, 1956 and 1957 – all three teams contained a sizeable home-grown influence, but that wasn't a surprise. As testimony to the work of Murphy, Whalley, Armstrong and many others, 26 teenagers were handed debuts throughout the 1950s, while numerous others, like Bill Foulkes, started out in their early 20s. Busby's vision was being realised. "I laid tremendous emphasis on building our own players," he said. "We went out on the highways and byways to find these young boys. We nurtured them, worked with them, coached them and looked after them. We were all together and you become a family." That made the next chapter in the story all the more devastating.

Few events define United quite like 6 February 1958. One word – Munich – can encapsulate almost everything that is United: history, honour, community, triumph in adversity, a sense of us against the world. That 23 people losing their lives in a plane crash is a tragedy is beyond doubt. But it is essential to consider the bond between players and public.

United regularly attracted crowds of 10,000 for FA Youth Cup matches during the 50s. The Reds met Wolves in the first two finals in 1953 and 1954, and in the first leg of the first final at Old Trafford, United won 7-1 in front of 21,000 supporters (the second leg ended 2-2, with United winning 9-3 on aggregate). The following year, the teams drew 4-4 at Wolves. Then David Pegg scored the winner from the penalty spot in front of 28,000 fans in Manchester. The public had watched these boys become men, but, on the cusp of becoming what many people were describing as potentially the best team in the world at the time, they were snatched away by a cruel twist of fate. It struck at the very heart of United: its young, promising players.

Many of the club's young players not on the trip to Belgrade for the European Cup quarter-final second-leg tie with Red Star stepped into the breach in the immediate aftermath. And every player since is taught about the history of United's young players and, in particular, the magnitude of the events of 6 February 1958. It's in the fabric of the club, part of the distinguished honour of wearing the shirt.

Inevitably, in order to rebuild, United had to buy players, such as Noel Cantwell, who joined United for £29,500 from West Ham in 1960, at the age of 28, and captained United to the restorative 1963 FA Cup Final win over Leicester City. But, again, youth would colour Busby's great team of the 1960s. In 1964 United won the FA Youth Cup for the sixth time. Seven of the starting 11 in the Final's 5-2 aggregate win over Swindon Town went on to play for United's first team, collectively amassing over 1,200 appearances. Five played a part in the squad during the 1968 European Cup winning season, and one of them was

George Best. The contributions of David Sadler (335 total appearances), John Aston Jnr (187) and John Fitzpatrick (147) are worth high commendation, but Best's 470 appearances and 179 goals only tell part of the story of his genius. He is perhaps the most naturally gifted talent United have ever produced. In the 1967-68 campaign he made 53 appearances (nobody played made more often), and scored 32 goals and won the *Ballon d'Or*.

A total of 14 of the 19 players who played that season had come through United's junior ranks, and in the European Cup Final at Wembley against Benfica, the Reds, playing in blue, won 4-2 with goals from Best, Brian Kidd (on his 19th birthday) and two from Charlton – all three were United youths – and the latter a Munich survivor. Some 10 years on, it was beautiful, bittersweet symmetry.

That United won the FA Youth Cup in 1964, but did not lift the trophy again until 1992, is perhaps telling about how the club's priorities had changed, particularly in the post-Busby era. United twice lost in the Youth Cup Final in the 1980s, but particularly in the 1970s, it was the changing of managers, the subsequent instability and the necessity to chase Busby's former glories that dimmed United's devotion to producing home-grown players. That continued until

Alex Ferguson arrived in 1986 and he set out to recapture United's reputation as a club with whom young players could make their name. It is undoubtedly the reason why Sir Matt Busby and Sir Bobby Charlton were supportive of Ferguson, despite his early struggles. They understood that this was a man who 'got' United. The success of the famed Class of '92 was a just reward for patience, and it remains an astonishing feat that has perhaps defined United's dominance of the Premier League era. But times have changed again since Giggs, Beckham, Scholes, the Nevilles and Butt first emerged.

If you were being ultra-critical of United's youth system today, you might point to a slowing conversion rate of Academy talents to first team stars. Only five home-grown players who made their debuts between 2000 and 2009 have gone on to make more than 50 appearances for United: Darren Fletcher, Kieran Richardson, Jonny Evans, Darron Gibson and Danny Welbeck. United would point to a restrictive and flawed Academy system in England, which recent changes have sought to address. The effects of that are as yet unknown, but it's worth noting that United give opportunities to more young players than ever before.

Consider these figures: in the 1950s United gave debuts to 26 teenage players. Six made 10 appearances or fewer, while collectively they played in 2,645 games (that figure would be much higher were it not for Munich). In the 60s, United debuted 20 teenagers, with just four players making 10 appearances or fewer, and collectively amassing 2,943 matches. In the 1970s, it was 22 teenage debutants, 10 players making 10 appearances or fewer and overall playing in 2,100 games. In the 1980s that figure dropped even more sharply: 14 teenage debutants, four making 10 appearances or fewer, and collectively racking up just 1,610 matches. In the 1990s, with Ferguson's plans in full swing, it was 29 teenage debutants (double the previous decade tally), with 13 players making 10 appearances or fewer, and going on to play in a mammoth 4,393 matches. In the 2000s, 38 teens made their United debut, 24 making 10 appearances or fewer, and overall playing in 1,624 matches.

It is necessary to reflect that in the 50s and 60s, substitutes were either non-existent or rare, squads were smaller and a group of 12 or 13 players might play the majority of the season's matches. So, that adds greater substance to those figures but, equally, it shows that the Academy now provides for a squad game. It also suggests that with United and other clubs granted greater freedom to attract the best young boys and give them the best coaching, quality will increase.

The reality is that United should, and hopefully will, always find a way of developing home-grown talent, because the intent to do so carries with it so much of the philosophy and identity of United's history and its future. Perhaps it is rooted in Munich, the tragic loss of young, promising lives, taken before their prime, and the sense of community it engendered; maybe it's the Mancunian way of being fiercely proud of your own; or possibly it's the specific story accompanying this history of producing young footballers that sets Manchester United apart from any other club in England. The intense pride in developing young players is not unique to Old Trafford, but the story behind why we value *our* young players definitely is.

Ben Hibbs is the former deputy editor of ManUtd. com and *United Review* and spent nine years working at Old Trafford. He is a freelance writer based in Manchester.

EIGHT

KING ERIC
BY SCOTT THE RED

ERIC CANTONA INSPIRED A generation of boys in Manchester and across the country to run around the playground at lunchtime, kicking a ball about, with the collars of their shirts lifted and their chests stuck out. Cantona was just cool.

Before the days when flicks and tricks were commonplace in England, Eric could regularly be seen strutting his stuff, showing off his fancy footwork and dazzling the crowd. He was a supremely talented footballer who had a wonderful first touch, and could score belters on the volley as well as he could with placed shots from distance, or with headers. His vision was spectacular and his creativity won us games.

Cantona came to United following a chequered past: his volatile nature had earned him enemies and had caused most clubs to overlook his talent because they couldn't handle the headache that he would almost certainly create.

When he was 20 years old, he retired from the French national team, calling the manager, Henri Michel, an "incompetent shit bag", after he was left out of the squad for a game against Czechoslovakia in 1988. He later apologised for his outburst, but this didn't stop the French FA banning him from playing for the national team for a year. Fortunately for Cantona, Michel was sacked soon afterwards following poor results and was replaced by Michel Platini who saw to it that the ban was rescinded.

While his international career was on the mend, however, his club career was about to take its first turn for the worst. After being substituted for Marseille, Cantona kicked the ball into the crowd and threw his shirt at the referee. They quickly shipped him off on loan to Bordeaux where he played well, but they wanted to get rid of him after claiming he repeatedly missed training. Cantona disagreed, insisting he had only missed training once, the day his dog died, but he was soon playing for Montpellier on loan. That club suspended him after Cantona overheard teammate Jean-Claude Lemoult criticising his performance, which resulted in Cantona throwing his boots at Lemoult's head. Cantona had played well though, and so the new Marseille manager, Franz Beckenbauer, requested that Cantona return to Marseille for the start of the following season. He scored seven goals in his first 12 games, but Beckenbauer fell out with the chairman and was sacked. Cantona then fell out with the replacement manager and was sold to Nimes, where he was named captain.

He was the same man he had always been, and after disagreeing with a referee's decision, threw the ball at him and stomped off the field before even seeing the red card that followed. Cantona was hauled in front of the disciplinary committee and banned for four games – a decision the striker obviously disagreed with. Cantona moved around the room, calling every man there an "idiot", one by one, before stalking out. His ban was increased to two months and he retired from football altogether, aged 25.

Fortunately, Platini managed to convince Cantona to change his mind, suggesting that a move to England might help his career. Gerard Houllier worked as an intermediary and a move to Sheffield Wednesday was soon on the cards. However, their manager, Trevor Francis, wasn't sure whether Cantona was worth the £1 million transfer fee, and therefore asked the player to join them on trial. Unfortunately, due to poor weather, the only way Francis could watch Cantona play was on an indoor pitch, so he asked for another week. Cantona refused to oblige and instead signed for Howard Wilkinson's Leeds United, who were top of the table.

By the time Cantona made his debut at the beginning of February, United were top of the league, but Eric soon helped to change that. Although he wasn't the star man at Elland Road to begin with, he contributed to Leeds' title win whereas United collapsed under the pressure. The fans there loved him, singing "ooh ahh Cantona" from the stands, with Cantona claiming his second consecutive league title winners' medal, having played the requisite number of games for Marseille the year before.

Cantona started the next season for Leeds with a 4-3 victory over Liverpool in the Charity Shield (the Frenchman scored a hat trick). It wasn't long, however, before cracks began to form in his relationship with Wilkinson. Cantona believed he was getting mixed messages from the manager. After leaving, Cantona revealed that fans told him they thought Wilkinson didn't like him because he was putting Wilkinson "in the shade".

"It became more and more clear that he wanted to get rid of me," Cantona said. "Wilkinson tried to explain his decision by peddling the rumour that I did not accept his authority and that he must be the only boss."

Thankfully, Sir Alex Ferguson believed he could bring out the best in the Frenchman, despite the number of managers who had failed before him, and after a phone call from Leeds chairman, Bill Fotherby, enquiring about signing Denis Irwin, Ferguson cheekily asked about the availability of Cantona. There was no deal for Irwin, but there was a meeting between Fotherby and Wilkinson, where they agreed to sell Cantona for £1.2 million.

Cantona has since reflected on the first time he met Alex Ferguson and why he decided to join United: "I remember my first meeting with Sir Alex when he wanted to sign me from Leeds, and in the first minute I knew that I had to work with the man. Of course, the name of Manchester United meant so much in football anyway, but I saw a man who wanted the same things that I wanted. He told me I could become a great player at United – and I believed in everything he told me. He is a man who has the same spirit as me. Looking back, he also saw the same philosophy in me that he saw in himself. We are football men. He was very special to me because he treated me like a man, not like a boy."

With Cantona, United were transformed from a team that were almost good enough to be the best to a team that would dominate English football. After winning the title with Leeds in his only season there, he guided United to our first league title in 26 years the following season, his third consecutive league title win with three different clubs.

However, it wasn't just Cantona's individual brilliance that made a difference, but the overall effect he had on our team, particularly the double-winning side of 1996. After being the catalyst for our success, for United winning back-to-back titles in 1993 and 1994, as well as winning the FA Cup, his defining season was 1995-1996. That is his legacy.

"You can't win anything with kids," Alan Hansen said on the opening day of that season, following United's 3-1 defeat to Aston Villa. Gary Neville, Phil Neville, Paul Scholes and Nicky Butt all started, with David Beckham and John O'Kane used as second-half substitutes. We had conceded the title to Blackburn the season before and the media didn't believe our young side had what it took to see off a new threat from Newcastle.

Cantona came back to the team in October 1995 for the Liverpool game, after serving his ban (for kicking a fan following his sending off against Crystal Palace the season before), and what a difference he made. He set up Butt's opening goal and then scored a penalty in the 2-2 draw and that set the tone for what would follow in the second half of the season. United went from 10 points behind on Christmas Eve to top of the table by the first week of March, after Cantona scored our only goal in a 1-0 win over Newcastle. He also scored the only goal of the game in our wins over West Ham, Arsenal, Tottenham and Coventry, as well as two goals in the 4-2 win over Wimbledon, a last-minute equaliser in a 1-1 draw with QPR and the opening goal in our 3-2 win over City, among others. It's hard to remember a time when a player has scored so many crucial goals in so many games.

With the help of 'the kids' that would apparently never win anything, as well as the experience of players like Pallister, Schmeichel, Keane, Irwin and Giggs, Cantona dragged us over the finish line, with us winning the league by four points.

The season wasn't over yet though – we had a day out at Wembley to look forward to first. After knocking out Sunderland, Reading, City, Southampton and Chelsea, only Liverpool stood in the way of us winning the double, our second in three seasons. After a drab game, Cantona's volley from the edge of the box managed to find its way through a crowded penalty area and into the back of David James's net, with less than five minutes to go. The image of him running to the crowd, grabbing his shirt, is enough to give any Red goosebumps.

What Cantona did that season wasn't merely a case of inspiring United to success; he also helped to turn our team of kids into a team of winners. Imagine if the likes of Beckham, the Nevilles, Scholes and Butt missed out on the title that year and didn't win any trophies. What impact would that have had on them as 21-year-olds, having to face the criticism from the press that they weren't up to the task; that Ferguson should never have believed they were capable of replacing proven talent like Hughes, Kanchelskis and Ince?

You would like to think they were mentally strong enough to overcome the disappointment regardless, but this talented bunch of youngsters started the following season believing they were capable of winning anything. They already had faith in their ability, but now this was proven beyond doubt by the medals they wore around their necks.

Two years after that next title in 1997, they won everything. The unprecedented Treble, the success that had eluded Liverpool despite their years of domination during the 1980s, was achieved by United. We won the league on the last day; we beat Newcastle in the FA Cup Final at Wembley, and overcame German champions Bayern Munich in the European Cup Final at the Nou Camp.

"I would have loved to have been on the pitch in Barcelona," Cantona said afterwards. He was no longer with the players he had inspired, having retired after that last league title in 1997, but there's no way of measuring the impact Cantona, and the success he helped achieve, had on them.

"It's difficult for a forward to be captain," Ferguson has said since. "Eric Cantona was such because he was an important influence to young players. They idolised him."

Although United were able to utilise Cantona's ability to bring in the trophies, his craziness and the outbursts didn't stop just because he was under the guidance of Ferguson. Cantona picked up six red cards in his time with the club but it was a night at Selhurst Park where he rode his luck too far.

Opposition players knew he would snap if they pushed his buttons, so that's exactly what Richard Shaw (who was voted Palace's Player of the Year that season) did, and he got what he wanted when

Cantona was sent for an early bath for a reaction to being constantly fouled. He turned down his collar and walked towards the tunnel, only for Crystal Palace fan Matthew Simmons to rush to the front of the stand and hurl abuse at Cantona (which later earned him a £500 fine for threatening language and behavior). "Fuck off, you motherfucking French bastard!" is what fans in the crowd report they heard. Having not regained his cool, Cantona flipped, diving into the crowd with a two-footed kung-fu kick, followed by a shower of punches.

Ferguson hadn't seen the incident (although this didn't stop him giving referee Alan Wilkie a mouthful at full time – forcing a police officer to intervene – blaming the referee for ignoring all the previous fouls on Cantona), he was too preoccupied with re-arranging the team, which was down to 10 men. That night he struggled to sleep; he rose in the middle of the night and watched the footage. His gut reaction was that Cantona's United career was over, but, thankfully, he had a change of heart.

Ferguson later recalled what happened in an interview with *L'Equipe* magazine: "The next day at breakfast, I told everybody: 'We're backing Eric. He's our player. The FA mustn't have his skin. He made a mistake. We all make mistakes.' Eric knew I was on his side. He knew he could count on me. He needed someone to help him, someone whom he could trust, who'd support him. I fulfilled this mission."

Cantona had the club on side (despite them suspending him for the rest of the season and fining him two weeks' wages) but the footballing authorities hadn't even started with him yet. He was stripped of the captaincy of the French national team; the FA increased his ban to eight months, and initially fined him £20,000 before increasing it to £30,000.

On the morning of the FA hearing, Paul Ince went to Cantona's hotel room, as he had also been charged with being involved in a melee with supporters following the kung-fu kick. He has since reflected on that morning, as reported in Philippe Auclair's book *Cantona: The Rebel Who Would Be King*:

"We stayed at the Croydon Park Hotel. We got up in the morning and I've got me suit on – the nuts, know what I mean? I knock on Eric's door and he's standing in a jacket, white shirt, long collars like that [he gestures to describe long, pointed collars], unbuttoned, so you can see his chest. 'Eric, you can't go to court like that', I told him and he says, 'I am Cantona, I can go as I want'."

The events at his disciplinary hearing may explain why Cantona's fine and ban were increased, as remembered by former FA executive director, David Davies in his memoir *FA Confidential*.

"I recalled a previous French FA hearing when Cantona smacked an official in the face," he said. "Anything was possible here. In perfectly good English, Eric delivered the most astonishing speech I've ever heard. 'I would like to apologise to the chairman of the commission,' Eric began. 'I would like to apologise to Manchester United, Maurice Watkins and Alex Ferguson. I would like to apologise to my teammates. I want to apologise to the FA. And I would like to apologise to the prostitute who shared my bed last night.' Had I honestly heard that? At least two members of the commission certainly hadn't grasped it. Cantona was taking the Mickey. He had to be."

Cantona was now 29 years old and it was clear that any of the misdemeanours earlier in his career could not be dismissed as acts of immaturity. He was just a bit crazy, he always had been, and we loved him for it. He is our hero and every mad story we hear about him adds to our admiration of him. Of course, all the memories of him on the pitch are the first things we think about when we call him a legend, but it is more than that. It's more than him being a great player with a bit of a mental side. Cantona got it. He knew how special it was to be a United player;

he understood how the fans felt about the club; he loved Manchester and he made us feel like he was one of us.

"I feel close to the rebelliousness and vigour of the youth here," he once said. "Perhaps time will separate us, but nobody can deny that here, behind the windows of Manchester, there is an insane love of football, of celebration and of music."

We *have* separated over time, and despite him repeatedly claiming that one day he will return to the club in some sort of official role, his trips to Manchester aren't very frequent. He does, however, make the effort to return on special occasions.

"AU REVOIR CANTONA AND MAN UNITED… COME BACK WHEN YOU'VE WON 18" read the banner at Anfield in the early 90s. In March 2010, United played Liverpool at Old Trafford for the first time since winning that 18th title, and Cantona was in the crowd, sharing in the celebrations at Carrington with the players following our 2-1 win.

Cantona left the club 15 years ago, but still the relationship is strong, with his name regularly being sung at Old Trafford. "I'm so proud the fans still sing my name," he said in 2004. "But I fear tomorrow they will stop. I fear it because I love it. And everything you love, you fear you will lose."

Finally, I'll leave you with words from a Cantona interview with Sky Sports that he gave four years ago. He was asked several questions about his time at United, and a clearly moved Cantona reflected on what Manchester United meant to him.

"In the last minutes of my life, I will have this club in my heart."

Eric Cantona gets it. He's one of us and we love him for it.

Scott the Red is a born and bred Mancunian who has been going to Old Trafford with his dad since before he can remember. He has a season ticket in the Sir Alex Ferguson stand. Scott created *The Republik of Mancunia* blog during the 2005-2006 season.

NINE

RED ARMY ON THE MARCH
BY BARNEY CHILTON

DESPITE THE DIVERSE LOCATIONS to have hosted Manchester United's European ventures, from the bland to the beautiful, both stadiums and cities, for the dedicated United fans whose endeavour, guile and dedication have made overcoming visa, travel, expense and ticket obstacles almost an art form, it can be the lure of the destination as much as the opponents that provokes pre-trip excitement.

After the tragedy of Munich and the glory of Wembley 10 years later, the decline of that great side led to eventual relegation, which meant that for much of the 1970s and 1980s United were a giant pressed outside the UEFA window, pawing to be let in.

We had to make do with sporadic European Cup Winners' Cup and UEFA Cup runs that, typical of the general malaise of the club, saw us peak in certain rounds. Though, to be fair, they still offered occasional unforgettable memories, like overcoming a 2-0 deficit at home to Barcelona in March 1984 as Bryan Robson's Captain Marvel impersonations left the Diego Maradona-led Barcelona shell-shocked in the last eight.

We continued to underachieve. Juventus were to knock us out in the semi-finals that year, but everyone still remembers that incredible quarter-final night. Indeed, it is often talked of as the greatest of United atmospheres. Which is all the more remarkable, as there have been many to choose from, dominated by those captivating European nights; like the Barcelona semi-final of 2008, when time seemed to stand still, even as Messi's movement did not. We urged the clock on after the Paul Scholes goal which was to prove the winner, while the team held off the Barcelona surges.

In Moscow (in ideal quiz-question fodder style, the final started on one date – 21 May 2008 – and ended on another (in the early hours of the 22nd)), we rid ourselves of the horrible hoodoo of penalty shoot-out knockouts and our almost farcical ability to replicate the England national side. Whether against Videoton (what a name) or Torpedo Moscow, only the Iron Curtain spared more general embarrassment at those spot-kick failures.

Although certainly United created miracle situations on a football pitch, there were other moments where you stood, chewing your nails, thinking, 'just do it one more time...please...' But still, there's an innate belief that stems from a manager, a feeling that at times anything was possible, however improbable.

Perhaps because it was John Terry and not just because of the banana slip (I remember clearly thinking it had gone in until the two lads either side of me lifted us all into a semi-orbit where our shins bounced on the plastic seats of the Luzhniki Stadium), but what he represents, that it is he who will always be remembered from that night. Ronaldo's header was powerful and instantly memorable, but you may struggle over time to remember who converted penalties for United (Tévez, Carrick, Hargreaves, Nani, Anderson and Giggs). And who can remember Anelka missing the vital sudden-death spot-kick that saw Van der Sar psyche him out as he aimed to the opposite side from where all the others had gone in. We had a new anthem "Viva John Terry, could have won the cup, but he fucked it up." And as Reds cried or cheered, embraced or ignored any symbolism, suddenly all the hassles and expense were forgotten – as they always are when it's good news. The European Cup Final of 2008 had been worth it all. As footballing culture changed, so did the Red Army on its travels. Where finance and travel restrictions during the early years of European football meant it was only a few close hangers-on who got the opportunity to travel (often with the team) by the time the 1968 European Cup Semi-Final away leg at Madrid came around, a dedicated few hundred made the unofficial journey to Spain.

By the 1970s, hundreds became thousands. They were not always appreciated, or well behaved, as highlighted by a blanket ban after fighting in St Etienne in 1977. The authorities moved the return leg to Home Park, Plymouth – in an attempt to stop any United fans from attending.

Society was changing. There was a great deal more access to travel, and the closed shop – as far as European away trips encouraged by the club – was dismantled, although this was not entirely appreciated by the powers that be. More and more United fans wanted to do what they were used to doing back home: travel by train, car, coach, hiking, any which way they could to see the matches. As recently as 1994, the club was silently hostile to United fans wanting to travel to these trips independently.

We have stumbled; we have had to bear ridiculous UEFA regulations, such as when Peter Schmeichel and a suspended Eric Cantona watched on next to him in the stands as Stoichkov and Romario destroyed us in the Nou Camp in 1994. We had to get to grips with the rules as much as a new style of playing, and perhaps because of that, naively our expectations until then were just to enjoy the journey itself. This was still new territory for Reds of a certain age, those who had grown up on tales of Porto and Ajax away in the 70s, now applauding an absolute hiding from Barcelona.

For all talk of our greed, we respect our European rivals. On the whole, United fans travel en masse and, while imbibing to staggering proportions, now generally behave well, taking pride in this Republik of Mancunia approach; a well-practised ability to enjoy rather than spoil any trip and hospitality. Indeed, despite the natural gutting nature of watching United lose two recent finals, in Rome and at Wembley to Barca, the behaviour of the United fans was admirable.

European away trips have thrown up some legendary stories. Witness Manchester United fans in Varna for the European Cup Winners Cup second-round tie

RED ARMY ON THE MARCH

during October 1983, as they saw Chairman Martin Edwards and a club delegation arrive for a Bulgarian folk evening in a nightclub already hosting scores of the travelling Red Army. This was at a time when our manager greeted travelling Reds with the rather unpleasant "What the eff are you lot doing here?" The club hierarchy didn't appreciate Reds intruding on their closed shop of 'trips for the boys'.

One Red present, Carl, described the scene: "The club party were all warmly clapped in by our party. Unfortunately for Martin Edwards, we had only got through our first course when his main dish arrived. An enormous food fight had erupted between our lot, which suddenly escalated with everybody throwing things in the direction of Mr Edwards!" As bread rolls bounced off his rather well groomed mane, one can only imagine his thoughts. "After things had quieted down, one or two of our sensible crowd used a bit of diplomacy with the Chairman. He saw the funny side of it and we left."

You can see why an adopted anthem in the bars around Europe for United fans has been: "If the Reds should play, in Rome or Mandalay, we'll be there ... but we'll be drunk, drunk, drunk as fucking skunks."

Thankfully, the tireless work of well-known United fan and fanzine founder Teresa McDonald meant the club were to finally reconsider their archaic approach of limiting tickets to fans travelling on their own trips, and a happy medium has been found. Now you can go how you like, with whom you like.

And then of course there is the football itself – the raison d'être to all that planning and buzz. The old romantic in me wishes the Champions League was still a knockout competition right from the off, but that doesn't suit the greed of the clubs or the TV companies who demand a certain script – at least until its very latter stages – to be played out again and again. It wasn't so long ago we actually had two group stages rather than the one. And the one has dulled.

The unknown element is long gone, and these days our European rivals are beamed into our living rooms, so we see them play live as much as we do our domestic opponents, and if there is a price to pay for that, it is that, tactically, teams start to morph into one state of being. The demands of the competition mean you only remember how far you got rather than how you got there. But it is the European nights which still get us going. We grew up with tales of Bestie's sensational El Beatle airport arrival, of that second leg against Bilbao. Redemption can also be found. Teddy Sheringham was castigated in Monaco one season as we limped to one of those frustrating eliminations that always haunt us more than even the finals lost (like Dortmund and Bayer Leverkusen). Yet, just a year and a bit later, he saved the day by enabling Ole's knee and flick. He was then serenaded with 'won the lot' as we were cheering him, lifting imagined trophies as he warmed up against Arsenal at Old Trafford.

It is still the date on the calendar we eye, the draw for the Champions League, both group and knockout stages. To us it will always be the European Cup, no matter what the suits and marketing men say, and while we can imagine what the Babes might have achieved had it not been for the tragedy, we will forever seek to uphold their manager's vision: "I wanted Manchester United to reach for the sky… the very nature of this tournament causes me to describe it as an adventure, which presented a challenge which had to be answered."

It is, and always has been, the tournament for Manchester United since Matt Busby forced through our invitation. Our histories are entwined; we dream of the next final. It has seen us travel near and far, to places we might never have noticed let alone visited (Kosice, Lodz…). It has given us memories that we treasure (Barca '84, and the game Fergie says is one of our top five performances – putting seven past Roma

– when with each attack, we scored!). It has seen some of the greatest players in Europe appear wearing the Red of United – and becoming European Players of the Year. It has seen Robbo hoisted on shoulders across Old Trafford after that comeback in '84 and David May jumping on a stepladder to get in on the celebrations like his grandad advised in '99. It is the silence of a shock elimination (or not making it out of the group stages), or the silence of nerves before a celebratory final whistle. Of checking for pasta under sauces, and of course the goals.

The goals: Ruud in Basel, Scholes in *that* semi, Rooney's understated debut with a hat-trick against Fenerbahce, 10 against Anderlecht and the first King of our two, King Denis, scoring nine goals in one European quest in '69, of Lennart Johansson, then UEFA President, saying as we watched Samuel Kuffour, inconsolable: "I looked out onto the pitch and I was confused. I thought, it cannot be, the winners are crying and the losers are dancing."

Alex Ferguson, after we played Barcelona in the 2-2 draw at Old Trafford in October 1994, talked of the "fantastic buzz about Old Trafford" and on such nights, we dream a little more than usual. The intensity of the competition means we rue certain failures, but all the big clubs do that, even Real Madrid.

"Europe runs deep in the psyche of Manchester United," Ferguson said recently. Every fan knows it, every trip shows it, every season proves it. We don't know how long it will last, those older Reds know all too well how time continues its relentless march. Where once you could touch your memories of '99, now it feels part of older reminiscences, alongside 'Sit Down' by James and the inspired 'Always look on the bright side of life' memories in the rain from Rotterdam in 1991. Cherished by us young 'uns as older Reds looked to '68 as *their* one. Asked after '99 why I still go, why the zeal for it all remains, I said: "Well, I want to do it all again." It might never be as good as '99, we knew that then, how could it be?, but it can be different, as Moscow showed. Another final won in quite remarkable circumstances. Possibly because of what Europe represents, ours is a script where fate sometimes gives us a welcome nudge. Call it kismet, call it what you will, but it's a tango that has given us spills, thrills and bellyaches.

Bobby Charlton talks of his, and the club's, incredible history; at times a saga, often a soap opera, but also a family. "The old man always told us that football is more than a game. It has the power to bring happiness to ordinary people... his belief was that Europe was the future."

Rio Ferdinand said after Moscow: "Sir Bobby was very emotional in the dressing room afterwards. The most poignant part of the night for me was Bobby coming up to me and saying: 'Well done. You deserved it.' You could see he was really pleased for the lads. Manchester United runs through his veins and he's an inspiration to all of us players, so it's great for us to be able to win the European Cup, particularly this year. Maybe it was written in the stars."

Whatever the cost, we did not recoil nor cease to embrace our dream. European football has always allowed us to look to the sky. To dream. And remember.

Barney Chilton has edited the first Manchester United fanzine, *Red News*, since 1987. His first game at Old Trafford was in 1976 and he's been romantically involved ever since; with the usual ups, downs, arguments and loving goonage.

TEN

TAKEOVER

BY JOHN-PAUL O'NEILL

29TH JUNE 2005, OLD TRAFFORD

10:30pm on a balmy summer evening and the new owners of Manchester United are under police protection as an angry crowd rains down missiles on a van ferrying them to safety away from the stadium. Officers on foot attempt to clear a path through barricades that supporters had hastily erected a few hours earlier, happily cracking a few heads with their truncheons along the way. The terrace song that had provided a backdrop to so many United

119

games as the takeover battle raged for most of the season – "How we kill him I don't know, cut him up from head to toe, all I know is Glazer's gonna die!" – had rung out all evening as the couple of hundred fans present make clear that, regardless of any share transactions which took place on the London Stock Exchange the previous month, this 127-year-old football institution still isn't the Glazers' to enjoy as they pleased.

NATURALLY, THE MEDIA RAN with the story in a big way: on their first visit to M16, United's new owners had been all but chased out of the area under a Greater Manchester Police escort. If this was what a 200-strong crowd could do in the closed season, what would it be like if they ever tried to attend a game? Former United star Arthur Albiston echoed the thoughts of many when he told the BBC, "I can't see Glazer or his sons actually turning up because the repercussions would be enormous." It was an understandable viewpoint, but hopelessly misplaced. Whilst to the outside world the television images of a midsummer riot at Old Trafford suggested as vibrant an opposition as ever, the reality was very different. If the evening's events had shown anything it was that, for all that a hefty portion of United's following had voiced their opposition to the takeover, only a tiny proportion were bothered about it enough to show up and demonstrate the dissent they'd pledged.

This was a last hurrah. The Glazers had come for Manchester United's pot of gold to take back to their Florida mansions and ultimately it had been handed over with barely a murmur. Come August, tickets at Old Trafford would still be sold out and a team in United's red would still be playing games of football, regardless of whether its owners – who once upon a time were made up of members of the Lancashire & Yorkshire Railway based in Newton Heath – now operated it solely as a cash cow.

The Glazers had got away with implementing their leveraged takeover, a ghastly scheme whereby they were allowed to borrow hundreds of millions of pounds to buy out the shareholdings, before flipping the debt onto United and securing it against the club's assets rather than their own, meaning that Manchester United was now saddled with an enormous bill and crippling interest rates for the dubious pleasure of being controlled by this dysfunctional family of weirdo American chancers. How had it ever come to this?

19TH MAY 2001, WHITE HART LANE

It's the last match of a season in which United had cantered to another championship triumph – the club's third in a row – but despite that success, two days earlier Alex Ferguson announced his intention to quit the club. Negotiations with the club's chief executive Peter Kenyon over a £1 million p/a post-retirement ambassadorial role had broken down and so Ferguson went public on MUTV: "All the talks on the subject are now dead. It is over. When my contract is finished I will leave United for good. I have decided I will not take any 'roving ambassador' roll and will sever all connections. – that's all there is to it. I am definitely going."

As the story developed there were plenty of off-the-record briefings evident in the weekend's press, amid mounting speculation that Ferguson's departure could actually be imminent. At that Sunday's game against Tottenham, United's support made clear where it stood on the issue, embarking on a twenty-minute unbroken rendition of "Every single one of us, loves Alex Ferguson" even as the team slumped to a 3-1 defeat.

This wasn't the first time Fergie had engaged in a high stakes gamble on his United future, having previously brought a dispute over an improved wage deal to a head in the build-up to the 1996 FA Cup final against Liverpool, when he threatened not to lead the team out. Ferguson came out on top in that spat and he would do so again here. The PLC eventually offered the pay increase he demanded for what was intended to be his final season in 2001/02, along with guarantees of the ambassadorial role he craved thereafter. With his future now secured, Ferguson was given greater access to the transfer kitty allowing the major purchases he sought.

After years of frustration when the PLC's parsimony had contributed to United missing out on top names such as Batistuta and Zidane, Fergie secured the budget he demanded and immediately went out and spent £28m of it on a player he'd long admired: Juan Sebastián Verón. The arrival of Verón, one of the biggest stars in Serie A, prompted previously unseen levels of giddiness amongst the club's support, with Fergie heralding the Argentine's arrival as the solution to the team's tactical problems following the previous two seasons' failures in Europe. Looking beyond the hype, a few observers wondered where Verón would actually fit into the team, but those concerns were minor compared to the wider questions subsequently raised regarding the transfer.

6TH FEBRUARY 2004, HEREFORD RACECOURSE

Majestic Moonbeam, a horse belonging to JP McManus, part of the 'Coolmore Mafia' group which owns a significant proportion of Manchester United, is lining up for the 4:20pm race during a quiet afternoon meet. Suddenly, a group of United supporters appears and invades the course, displaying banners that warn "Quit The Horseplay Coolmore". The protest is in response to the controversy which had been stoked up in the wake of the dispute between Alex Ferguson and his one-time Coolmore associates - the Irish millionaires McManus and John Magnier - that is largely being conducted through the affairs of Manchester United. The message is simple enough: mess about with our club and we'll find ways to mess about with you. A subsequent statement makes clear that further races featuring Coolmore's steeds will be targeted, but the fans' action is far from a simple matter of defending the club's manager from attack; another significant investor called Malcolm Glazer is also mentioned as the group looks to check the advances of the ever increasing number of speculators eyeing up the club solely for financial gain.

Ferguson's disagreement with McManus and Magnier centred on the ownership of Rock Of Gibraltar, a racehorse in which the Irishmen had gifted Ferguson a share – allowing it, moreover, to run in Ferguson's colours. It showed great promise and a record seven consecutive Group One race wins swiftly followed before it was retired to stud, with breeders paying fortunes for the right to rear one of its progeny. Ferguson believed his association with the horse entitled him to half of the millions those stud rights would generate, a claim Coolmore contested. Legal action ensued.

Coolmore had steadily been buying into United and, as the row escalated, were now the biggest single investors in the club.

Through their shareholding they could apply pressure on Ferguson by questioning the plc board about his management of the club. To that end they hired the private investigations firm Kroll and set about digging. The result was a list of 99 questions, submitted to United's chairman Roy Gardner in January 2004. Answers were sought to all manner of issues relating to the management of the club, with a particular focus on monies passed to agents employed in the club's transfer dealings.

Since Verón's move in 2001 these payments had rocketed, with a number of the deals involving the so-called 'super agent' Pini Zahavi. Meanwhile, there was also concerns about a conflict of interest with Ferguson's own son Jason who was now in the business of representing players. By early 2004 concern at the scale of the payments flooding out of the club was growing. Each transfer commission paid to an agent equated to the value of hundreds, if not thousands, of season tickets – hard earned money handed over by fans who expected it would be used to improve the team. Signings such as Eric Djemba Djemba, Kleberson and David Bellion were clearly not doing that - just the opposite in fact - whilst fees paid for other signings such as Diego Forlan and Cristiano Ronaldo were higher than the selling clubs had previously come close to agreeing with other suitors such as Middlesbrough and Arsenal respectively. After an internal review, United denied any impropriety and released a statement saying, "The review has not identified the redistribution of any payment to anyone employed or connected with the club. However, in the future, to ensure we protect the club from such allegations, we will ask for a declaration from the agent that they have no direct or indirect relationship with anyone at the club".

For some reason Coolmore obviously believed that focusing on these issues could help in their attempts to force Ferguson to back down over Rock Of Gibraltar and incredibly, it appeared to have a swift effect. Fergie soon withdrew his claim to fifty per cent of the stud rights and on Sunday 7th March released a statement asking United supporters not to carry out their threat of disrupting the Cheltenham Festival later that month, an action that had been mooted as a further attempt to pile pressure on Coolmore. Whilst some observers reasonably enough wondered what Kroll might possibly have turned up that could force such a stubborn and legendary grudge-bearer into so humiliating a public U-turn, Fergie himself would later simply comment, "Grown men move on." Perhaps so, but it came as news to many in football.

23RD AUGUST 2005, BUDAPEST AIRPORT

United's flight has just arrived in Budapest for the club's Champions League qualifier against Debrecen and the players are filing through the arrivals hall. A couple of supporters have spotted Alex Ferguson and are questioning him on his role during the previous spring's takeover battle. "You've fucked us over, you could've spoken out about it," insists one of the pair, to which Fergie hits back, "I've got close mates who've been working with me here for fifteen years, they come first in all this." The supporter isn't impressed. "So don't the fans come first?" Fergie is reeling. "Well, I suppose they do come somewhere." This doesn't impress the chap who's spent a fortune travelling to Hungary to see what is effectively a meaningless game following the comprehensive first leg result a fortnight earlier. "You what? That's well out of order!" he blasts. Fergie, clearly unused to such insubordination, has had enough, "Well if you don't like it go and watch Chelsea."

Fergie's line about having close mates to consider would have sounded familiar to a handful of Reds. Two days after the Glazers bought out Coolmore's stake in United a small impromptu gathering took place at the home of Andy Walsh – leader of the Independent Manchester United Supporters Association when it successfully opposed BSkyB's bid for United in 1998 – and he was encouraged to try and revive his line of communication with Ferguson which the latter had opened during that earlier takeover battle. If there was any hope left that the Americans could still be stopped it lay with the manager and what he might do now.

The Glazers had seemed defeated for good in November 2004 but since they resurfaced in February word had continually leaked that Ferguson would be the key to any deal. The banks saw him as the figure who brought United success and that success is what brought the money rolling in, so when the Glazers went looking for funds to finance their bid the banks wanted guarantees that the management structure would remain in place. Effectively, "Get Ferguson and you'll get the money."

The only public utterance United's manager had made on the whole Glazer issue had come back in November when, with the Americans' initial approach comprehensively knocked back, he had come out with some platitude about the club being better off in supporters' hands. During the Sky battle he'd been similarly circumspect, largely keeping schtum in public but privately encouraging Walsh.

Back to 2005 and a handful of Reds privy to news of a telephone conversation between Walsh and Ferguson arrived at Walsh's house, eager to hear what had transpired. Walsh was far from upbeat and relayed the conversation. "He says he's only got a couple more years left and that he's got too many staff who he feels responsible for to quit now."

Funny that there'd been no hint of such selflessness back in 2001 when Ferguson was looking out for his own finances; now it was the club's that were at stake things were evidently very different. There's no doubt that Ferguson will have fully understood what the takeover meant for Manchester United – after all, he didn't even have to look outside his own immediate family for expert financial advice – and he would have been equally aware through his network of contacts that his refusal to sanction the Glazers' move at any point in the preceding months would have killed it off instantly. Despite that, he'd chosen to adhere to Stock Exchange rules which supposedly prevented him from speaking out, even though the FA's equivalent had never managed to prevent him speaking his mind.

Walsh went on to become the General Manager of a new football club – FC United of Manchester - set up as a direct protest against the Glazers' takeover and starting life in the tenth tier of English football in August 2005. Despite their lowly beginnings, they've appeared in Ferguson's sights far more than might be expected. During a press conference in January 2008 Ferguson hit out after journalists had dared ask for his views on the latest spat between fans and the club. "You go to people who think they're the conscience of this club, who are not the conscience of this club. People like independent supporters association or FC United. They're not the conscience of this club, no way." A couple of months earlier, Ferguson had responded to the Sports Minister Gerry Sutcliffe's criticism of ticket prices, "It's unfair and inaccurate ... I do not understand why he is picking on Manchester United ... he can go and watch that mob United FC," whilst in an official United diary of the 2005/06 season he referred to the people behind FC United as "self-publicists" and claimed that he'd been bombarded by calls from anti-Glazer supporters asking him to quit. "They seemed to forget that I have brought at least ... well, I've brought everybody here! I said 'What happens to my staff if I go?' I feel that I have a responsibility to them." Walsh has never publicly responded to any of Ferguson's comments. When it comes to talk of the Glazers and Manchester United's conscience, he's probably just content that at least he did his bit.

10TH MARCH 2010, OLD TRAFFORD

United have just qualified for the Champions League quarter-finals after dismantling AC Milan 4-0. The Italian side included David Beckham in his first competitive outing at Old Trafford since he left for Madrid seven years earlier. Long after his team-mates have left the pitch he milks the acclaim from the home fans and, as he walks towards the Stretford End, takes a green and gold scarf being offered by a supporter. A huge roar goes up and Beckham wraps the scarf around his neck before saluting the crowd one last time and heading down the tunnel.

The Glazers' bond issue prospectus, released in early January 2010, allowed many United supporters the chance to fully understand the scale of the cost the club had borne under the Americans' ownership: in less than five years the total was already running at well over £400 million. Meanwhile, hidden away in the 322-page prospectus were details of schemes that would allow the Glazers to extract £20 million from the club each year from 2010 to 2017, and up to another £95 million at any time they chose. The whole cost to Manchester United including dividend payments over the seven years had the potential to be in excess of £500 million above the amount the Glazers were seeking to borrow from investors in the first place. Despite that, Alex Ferguson's verdict on this latest wheeze from the club's "wonderful owners" was that "The bond issue is a good thing for the club. There is debt there but it has never interrupted my plans for the team at any stage. I don't have any concerns about the financial situation. I have absolutely no issue at all with the club's finances." The bond prospectus itself was slightly more forthcoming, warning ominously, "Our significant indebtedness could adversely affect our financial health."

One fan's suggestion of the adoption by supporters of green and gold – for a brief time the colours of Newton Heath FC – as a way of signifying opposition to the Glazers was wonderfully simple and brilliantly effective, and tens of thousands quickly took it up. Even Ferguson, usually so dismissive of dissenters to the Americans' regime, realised this was too big for him to tackle head on so he tried another tack. Acknowledging fans' right to protest, he insisted that "I cannot let it interfere with my direct route to winning the title or the European Cup. That's the only thing that concerns me."

The implication was clear, but Fergie shouldn't have worried. The green and gold 'plan' had one vital flaw: there was no plan. Once everyone wore it, what then? The Glazers had come for money, not popularity. By the time Beckham wrapped that scarf around his neck, green and gold at Old Trafford wasn't news. David Beckham in green and gold was, but only for about five minutes until he distanced himself as far from it as possible in a post-match interview. "To be honest, it's [the anti-Glazer protest] not my business. I'm a United fan and I support the club. I always will.

It's nothing to do with me how it is run." And who could criticise Beckham for that? After all, it was the same stance so many others had adopted before him. Whereas in 2005 it had been songs and protests, in 2010 it was scarves and protests. A mere fad for a brief time. When the games came round the ground was still full, the team played on, Fergie backed the Glazers, and they counted the money.

10TH AUGUST 2012, NEW YORK STOCK EXCHANGE

The bond issue of 2010 has proved but a stop-gap. Ever more desperate for cheap finance to reduce the cost of the loans they'd secured against United, the Glazers had seen proposed share issues in Singapore and Hong Kong fall through and now they're in New York. The city's Stock Exchange almost looks like it's been turn into Old Trafford's megastore for the day with traders dressed in the team's shirts and the club's crest displayed on huge drapes – all part of the hype as United's Initial Public Offering (IPO) is launched. Shares are priced $6 below what the Glazers hoped they might attract but there's still enough demand to raise $233 million – half of which goes straight into the Glazers' pockets.

The IPO prospectus was released the previous month and included details of an "Equity Incentive Award Plan" designed to reward senior United employees with benefits from a share scheme worth up to £204 million. When questions were asked whether those beneficiaries would include the club's manager, Ferguson angrily hit back. "In regards to suggestions that I have praised the Glazer family because I stand to financially benefit from the proposed IPO, there is not a single grain of truth in this allegation. I do not receive any payments, directly or indirectly, from the IPO." But then no-one ever suggested he would. What they wanted to know about was the Equity Incentive Award Plan. In New York for the IPO launch, David Gill was interviewed on Sky News and asked whether he would gain from the Award Plan. His answer was intriguing. "There is an executive share scheme but the details of that are yet to be decided."

The cost to United of having the Glazers as owners now stands at over £530 million but Ferguson still insists "I am comfortable with the Glazer situation. They have been great." At the same time the Glazers' own IPO prospectus warns United's debts "could adversely affect our financial health and competitive position." But what else can Ferguson now say? His position is irretrievably tied into their regime. Tourists flock to sit in the Sir Alex Ferguson stand and take pictures of the Sir Alex Ferguson statue; four huge banners depicting Sir Alex Ferguson drape down the outside of one side of the ground - a Stalinist dictator might think it all a bit much. Sir Matt Busby certainly would. In 1973 he wrote, "Some admirers asked me if they could commission a bust for me to go on permanent display at Old Trafford. I said no. Because my memorial is the three great teams I created for Manchester United." That only changed after he died in 1994 but the Glazers need to cash in now and recognise the value of Ferguson to the United 'brand' just as much as those bankers did back in 2005.

To the vast majority of supporters Alex Ferguson can do no wrong. To them his trophy-winning record supersedes everything else, easily overcoming any distaste at his support for the Glazer regime. After all, they point out, look where we were before Fergie came along. And it is fair comment, if trophies are your only measure of a club. Who can argue with his twelve league championships triumphs? But for others, the constant rises in the cost of tickets under the Glazers, the lifelong fans priced out of going to games, the local youngsters who don't even contemplate going to Old Trafford, the unsustainable levels of debt - it all suggests a club with a worrying, uncertain future, especially when moneybags Manchester City now rule the local perch.

John-Paul O'Neill has travelled to over 40 different countries to watch United and has been a regular contributor to Red Issue since 1995, as well as having written for *United We Stand*, *Red News*, United's official club magazine and programme (pre-Glazer), *The Independent* and *FourFourTwo*.

ELEVEN

SOFA SURFING
BY DARREN RICHMAN

IT IS PART OF me now. Over a decade on and snippets of the commentary still float to the surface of my mind at least a dozen times a day. Standing in a queue for a cashpoint: "Can United score? They always score." Half asleep in the shower, "Giggs with the shot… Sheringham!" Bored at the cinema, "Name on the trophy." I'd love to say my subconscious foists Shakespearean monologues upon me without warning, or sage advice from family members, or even simply lines from pop songs. But no, apropos of nothing, any hour of the day, I am liable to think of Clive Tyldesley: a warm shiver runs up my spine, and I smile. It remains the one thing guaranteed to raise the hairs on the back of my neck merely by its recall. This sensation even occurred just now as I typed those bits of commentary, a Proustian memory of childhood happiness. 14 years old. Wednesday, 26 May 1999.

I have been fortunate enough to attend some pretty memorable United games over the years. The good (5-3 at White Hart Lane from 3-0 down; Beckham from the halfway line against Wimbledon, 4-3 City; 8-2 Arsenal), the bad (surrendering a 40-year unbeaten home record in Europe against Fenerbache on my first midweek trip; 1-6 City), and the ugly (Eric's kung-fu kick on Matthew 'it's-an-early-bath-for-you' Simmons; any game involving Luke Chadwick). Despite these experiences, I have still watched the large majority of the games in my life from the living room. For me, football viewing is a pursuit that requires concentration. Therefore, I would always opt for the lounge over a lager, pubs doing little for me on a match day.

I was a season ticket holder by the time United reached another Champions League final. My father and I went to Moscow in 2008, and though the day would certainly make an appearance in any list of my top five ever, there can only be one candidate for the top. Moscow was more recent and I was in attendance, yet '99 remains the most vivid, a day never to be bettered, one that I can recall with perfect clarity.

My dad did try to get tickets. He was quoted ludicrous prices that suddenly didn't look quite so ludicrous at 9.45 on the evening of the game. In the end, we watched it as we had so many times before, in the living room with our pals Gary and Mark (closest friends since they met at school in the mid-60s and kicked a stone along the ground insisting they both got to be Bobby Charlton). Given that this was how we watched the vast majority of United's games in the 90s, it somehow seems fitting that we should have failed to land tickets. Gary, as always, brought a chocolate orange.

Since the advent of Sky, Gary has joined us for all televised United games. A heady mix of polite and superstitious, he brought an orange (as we have come to refer to them) to the first one in '92 (United won) and he has continued to do so ever since. Football, like life, is a thing over which we have little control despite constant attempts to kid ourselves otherwise. I have the unique responsibility of deciding when the orange is opened depending on how the game is going. By way of a rough guide, if the game is 0-0 then it will usually be opened around the hour mark, when Sir Alex might think about a substitution. If United go behind, then we will open it earlier. Everyone must have at least one slice. The good people at Terry's have got Fergie out of a lot of tight jams over the years, without receiving a single word of thanks. As a side note, Gary is the same man who stages mock Champions League draws in his kitchen using pots and pans. He adheres to all the appropriate stipulations regarding grouping, and can narrow United's possible opponents down to a miniscule shortlist on the eve of the actual draw itself. In brief, we are not normal.

I used to joke that, being born and raised in North London, naturally I am a Manchester United fan. This was largely a defence mechanism, attacking myself before the usual glory-hunting accusations that were only ever refuted with a quick airing of my childhood photographs from the late 80s in a United strip. In truth, I have known very few United fans around my age worthy of the name. At school there were none. One boy, not untypically, claimed he was only interested in televised games. When I asked him how he followed Saturday games at 3pm, he casually informed me: "Saturday games aren't important." We never spoke again.

At school I came to epitomise all things United. Teachers would mock me if their team had beaten mine (Mr Middleton, a West Ham fan, memorably said I looked like Barthez when I put my hand up to answer a question in double chemistry the day after that ill-fated attempt to put Di Canio off). Friends understood that my moods were determined by the weekend's fixtures, and I generally became a focal reference point for the world's greatest football club. United might be the most well-supported team on earth, but you wouldn't have known it in this leafy suburb, and I considered my role an ambassadorial one. I wore my status like a badge of honour. A friend told me years later that my inability to stomach any criticism of the club reminded him of Gary Neville. I believe it was aimed as a barb but I can think of no greater compliment.

That day, the only concession I publicly made to the magnitude of the occasion was the flag I had stashed away in my bag. Red, white and black, and emblazoned with the legend, 'Champions League Final 1999', it had been purchased on a recent trip to Old Trafford. I boarded the school bus alone that evening. I have no memory of the whereabouts of my friends, but I can recall precisely what happened next. I made my way to the back of the vehicle, a tactic unheard of if you weren't in the upper years, and utterly without precedent in my school career up to that point. I retrieved the flag and draped it over the glass with pride when the driver of the bus behind ours caught my eye. Expecting the finger, I was delighted with the three he gave me. He pointed at me as if to say 'you', which in this instance translates as 'United' then held up two fingers on one hand and one on the other. 2-1 United. Simple really. I could have saved myself an awful lot of bother if I'd just trusted him and had an early night.

Perhaps the enormity of the day clouds my memory, but I recall another period of solitude once I arrived home from school. I don't recall seeing my brother or sister. I have no idea where my mum was. It's possible they were around and I was just lost in my own world of anxiety. The same might be true of my friends on the bus. No English team had been in the European Cup Final since Heysel, at which time I was barely a few months old. Nothing could be left to chance. I made my way into the living room and did something rather strange.

I approached the mantelpiece and placed two significant belongings beneath the print of Monet's, *Bridge over a Pool of Water Lilies*. First up was the bottle of Manchester United wine we had purchased on one of my very first trips to Old Trafford. Originally a tongue-in-cheek purchase from the Megastore, somehow over the years it was decided that this bottle was only to be opened in the event of United winning the European Cup. The second item was a miniature figurine of our Lord and Saviour, Eric Cantona. It was at this point that the madness set in.

I am not a religious person. I don't attend synagogue, nor do I pray. I am inclined, however, to make various deals with God – the God whose very existence I doubt. I am 27 years old, I cannot recall the last time someone told me to 'make a wish' and I didn't opt for United to win the Premier League or the European Cup. Another favourite technique is to barter with God during a long and sleepless night. I let him know that it's OK for, say, a situation with a girl not to work out, if it means United will triumph. As with any relationship, there has to be a bit of give and take.

To this day I have no idea why I did what I did next. Given my constant dialogue with the Lord, I am clearly not a staunch and fearless atheist. Bearing this in mind, I put on a yarmulke and the tallis I had not worn since my Bar Mitzvah and began to recite the Shema to Eric Daniel Pierre Cantona. It is the only prayer I know by heart (well, the first few lines) and many consider it the most important part of any service. The first verse captures the monotheistic essence of Judaism with the refrain 'Hear, O Israel: The Lord is our God, the Lord is one.'

To the casual observer I might have looked like any orthodox Jew praying at the Wailing Wall, but in place of one of the most sacred sites on earth was a six-inch poor likeness of a French centre forward. What on earth possessed me? Why did I think this was anything like appropriate? A prayer highlighting the essential tenet of Judaism – that there is only one God – and there I was desecrating Commandments two and three in one fell swoop (You shall have no other Gods before me. You shall not make yourself an idol.) Fortunately, it was Eric, and I recalled with some relief that one need only fear false idols. Still, given the outcome, if there is someone upstairs, then I can safely say he doesn't bear a grudge. Or, more likely, just as many of us had always suspected, Eric is God. Not for nothing was his nickname simply 'Dieu'.

Come kick-off, we opted for a conventional 4-3-1 formation with myself, my dad, Gary and Mark closest to the TV, the Arsenal-supporting contingent of my brother, mother and grandfather were in the cheap seats, and my sister upstairs in her bedroom. There was a rare, unspoken belief that nothing could possibly go wrong. The Champions League music played. I felt proud and privileged in equal measure. We were on the brink of the treble, not bad for a team that qualified as runners-up in the league the previous season.

Mario Basler opened the scoring for Bayern Munich in the sixth minute, but that was OK; we never make it easy for ourselves and assorted other clichés. Time ticked away as is its wont. It is a truth universally acknowledged that the clock ticks faster when your team is behind. United hardly threatened. Half-time came and went. Nothing changed. Bayern hit the woodwork twice. The chocolate orange was opened. We silently ate our slices. Sheringham and Solskjaer were brought on. My grandfather, Zigi (a genial Holocaust survivor), nonchalantly declared "they'll both score" in a futile bid to lift our spirits. It was the second accurate prediction of the day, though I viewed it with weary scepticism. Lothar Matthäus, arguably the greatest ever German footballer, was substituted with four minutes remaining, and arrogantly conducted the Bayern fans like an orchestra. The Champions League is the only major trophy that eluded this titan of the game. I believe the word is hubris.

Mark had given up. Having spent the second half perusing magazines (a superstition designed to indicate he no longer cared about the outcome and lull the fates into a false sense of security), he now declared: "I think it was just one game too many." Past tense. Gary later claimed that in his heart he still felt we had a chance, but I know I was inclined to agree with Mark's fatalism. For all the magic of the campaign, we just weren't creating anything.

Out of nothing we won a corner. United had scored in every single Champions League game that season. This was a different time, an era when Beckham was still routinely abused up and down the country off the back of his red card at the World Cup. He was also in the form of his life. Peter Schmeichel, the greatest goalkeeper in the club's history playing one last time for the champions, came forward, just as he had so many times over the years in times of need. We were all standing by this point. Please United. *Please*. One last big push.

A cross, a failure to clear, a mishit shot from Giggs and then – as you probably recall – Teddy Sheringham equalised. Pandemonium. A sound emerged from my lungs somewhere between a squawk and a song. I raced round the coffee table and down the hall. Everyone was running and hugging and screaming. My dad later informed me that he and Gary had gone to hug and had failed to coordinate the move properly in their excitement, the result being that their heads came together in a near-kiss. The commentator said "name on the trophy" but none of us heard. We didn't need to hear. We all knew. Tears rolled down my cheeks. My mum tried to calm me down but it was pointless. It remains the only time I have cried with joy. The Flaming Lips were right, 'happiness makes you cry.'

The next thing I can recall I was back in the lounge and United had another corner. A blur. Solskjaer! The camera cut to and fro. First we saw a dumbfounded Matthäus on the bench. Then Schmeichel celebrated with a cartwheel, a skill I can only assume he was saving for a special occasion, as he'd never done it before. Samuel Kuffour wept as openly as a sportsman ever has in defeat, beating the ground in frustration. Sir Bobby Charlton grinned and poked his tongue through his teeth like a schoolboy. Our own celebrations were marginally more restrained than for the first goal. I think we all knew from that point on that there could be only one outcome. Even the spectre of the golden goal held no fear once we'd equalised. In the words of assistant coach Steve McClaren: "I don't think this team ever loses, it just runs out of time."

Gary somewhat typically insisted, "we can still blow this." I'm still not sure whether this was a joke, pessimism or simply a bid to keep fate onside for those final few seconds. If the latter, he needn't have bothered since Collina could barely rouse the Bayern players from the floor to take the centre, let alone mount an attack. A few seconds later he blew the final whistle and triggered the third riotous celebration in as many minutes. As *The Sun* would have it on Thursday morning, '*Our subs sink Germans*'.

While Reds all over the globe were celebrating with beer or champagne, we were knocking back the official Manchester United red wine. It was pretty disgusting but boy did it taste sweet. A mere glance at the empty bottle in front of me as I type brings a smile to my face. There was much to ponder in those minutes that followed.

Less well documented is the fact that ITV cut to an advert break during the celebrations and ceased broadcasting altogether for about half an hour after the game ended. Thinking fast, we switched over to RTL (the channel we'd watched the Bayern group games on since British TV didn't yet show all English Champions League games as a matter of course). It was a surreal juxtaposition with the jubilation on ITV as we witnessed a succession of distraught players interviewed, my grandfather and mother on translation duties. They were all 'sick as a parrot' or words to that effect.

David May memorably hogged the limelight and soaked up the acclaim. I often hope those photographs will be placed in a time capsule and football historians of the future will just assume that's Beckham or Giggs.

Two things of note happened the next day. Firstly, I turned to my friend Marc in maths and said: "It's a strange sensation, the realisation that there is no chance things will ever be this good again." The thought didn't depress me; it was simply a statement of fact. That truly was as good as it could possibly get. A season that special deserved a dramatic denouement and we got that and then some. George Best probably didn't have many regrets, but leaving his seat in the Nou Camp with a few minutes remaining has to go down as an error. Still, he scored in a European Cup Final so I guess we can call that 1-1.

The other noteworthy incident involved my grandmother. Zigi's wife, Jeanette, has absolutely no interest in sport whatsoever. She has never watched a game in her life. That morning when she turned on the television and saw that Manchester United had made history and were the main story on the news, she cried. She had no idea what any of it meant but knew how happy it must have made her son-in-law and grandson. That is the definition of unconditional love. That is how I feel about United.

Darren Richman's writing has appeared in *The Huffington Post*, *The Independent on Sunday* and *The Guardian*. He co-writes the biweekly Smudger Smith column for *The Independent* and currently has a feature film in development with Big Talk Productions and Studio Canal. Darren supports Manchester United and a woman's right to choose.

TWELVE

OLD TRAFFORD EVOLUTION
BY ANDY MITTEN

YOU COULD SEE FLOODLIGHTS from my bedroom window on the Stretford/Urmston border and I convinced myself that they were Old Trafford's floodlights. When they came on at night, I imagined Bryan Robson and Steve Coppell bathed in this brilliant artificial light, thrilling thousands of adoring fans.

They were actually the floodlights of a freight terminal in Trafford Park. They still stand by the Trafford Centre, but once I learned their true role, I convinced myself that I could *hear* Old Trafford from my home on a match day. And I could. It was only for the biggest games in the 80s, but, with a fair wind, the roar was unmistakable from two miles away.

How I longed to go and be part of that crowd, but my dad wouldn't take me to see United. He played semi-professionally himself and every Saturday (United used to play every Saturday), from the age of three, I went with him to a match; to Salford City and Stalybridge Celtic, Hyde United and Northwich Victoria, but never to Old Trafford. "I'll take you when you're older son," he'd say.

Someone else beat him to it. One day at school, Jason Turner told us that he was allowed to take his five best mates to Old Trafford for a league game as a birthday present. I was invited. And so, on 7 May 1984, aged 10, I went to Old Trafford for the first time (a defeat to Ipswich Town). A group of primary school mates walked past the real Old Trafford floodlights and behind the real Stretford End. The ground was unprepossessing and not as big as I expected –unsurprising given that the lower tier is below ground level.

The impact was different once through the turnstiles. We went in the Stretford Paddock, a part wooden terrace that held 8,000, wedged between the Stretford End proper and the main stand.

I've been fortunate to travel widely with football and see many of the world's great wonders, yet that first sight of the vivid green pitch remains the greatest thing I've seen in my life. It's the only thing that has ever truly taken my breath away – though seeing the mighty Mississippi River in flood around St Louis came close.

It was mesmerising to see the Old Trafford pitch for real. Maybe all football fans feel the same when they first visit their club's home, but the aura and grandeur was immense. The pitch seemed brighter and smaller than on television but, unlike the stands, which surrounded it, perfect. Old Trafford was an incongruous mixture of old and new in 1984 – the roof I was standing under dated back to the 1920s. Out of that dark stretched the pitch, manicured and lush, a fecund oasis in the middle of the decayed Trafford Park, where dad worked.

The ground was unique among British stadia because it was developed to a master plan – the first part of which commenced when it was built by the country's leading stadium designer, Archibald Leitch, in 1908. The second was set out by chairman Louis Edwards in the 60s, working with Manchester architects Atherden Nutter. The original master plan shaped the Old Trafford we see today, with a logical progression throughout the last century.

This foresight was unmatched by any other British football ground. Look at Anfield, White Hart Lane,

Highbury, Goodison, St James's Park, The City ground, Villa Park and more. Look across the city towards Maine Road, which was developed piecemeal with uneasily juxtaposed stands of varying styles and sizes, designed by different architects.

Old Trafford was designed to allow it to keep growing. The stadium held 80,000 when it opened, the construction funded by United's chairman, the brewer JH Davies. With three sides of terracing and a seated multi-span main stand designed by Leitch, it was the grandest stadium in football. That main stand wasn't Leitch's greatest structure – that resides at Ibrox – but the tunnel remains.

United couldn't afford to develop Old Trafford as they had hoped. The team were not always successful, and were relegated in 1931, with average gates of just 12,000. Crowds fluctuated wildly, and by the 1930s other teams had started to build double-decker stands and covered terraces. Old Trafford appeared outdated. The main stand was bombed by the Luftwaffe in 1941, and for four years after the war, the Reds played at Maine Road. Old Trafford wasn't considered as grand as Goodison or White Hart Lane; when the Stretford End was covered in 1959, the roof design reflected the worst of the 1920s, with numerous poles obstructing the view. Two years later, Sheffield Wednesday unveiled an innovative cantilevered stand, far in advance of anything seen by the banks of the Manchester Ship Canal. As a result of this, Hillsborough was chosen as a venue for the 1966 World Cup.

Old Trafford was fortunate to get the nod ahead of Maine Road as the Manchester venue, but United only got the green light on the condition that the stadium could offer more seats. In 1964, the ground had just the 8,000 main stand seats, plus 1,500 more bench seats at the back of the Stretford End that had been paid for by supporters in 1962.

The World Cup provided fresh impetus for the development of the second master plan. The United Road terrace was replaced by a cantilever stand with terracing for 10,000 at the front and 10,000 seats behind. At the back of the stand was a strip of 55 five-seater executive boxes, the reaction to which was initially negative. United's directors wondered who would like to watch football from behind glass, while Bobby Charlton was taken to task for calling the improved stadium "The Theatre of Dreams".

The next change at Old Trafford was the erection in 1971 of fences on all four sides, a step considered necessary in order to contain the increasing problem of hooliganism. United declined on the pitch in the early 70s but, conversely, the ground was at its loudest and

United's support had become a phenomenon. People talked about the fans ahead of the players. Even when the club were relegated to the second division in 1974-75, United's average home gate was 48,389 – 2,000 more than the best-supported first division side that season, Liverpool. The Stretford End was renowned for its atmosphere and scientists measuring the noise level stated that it was equivalent to a 747 at take-off.

"It was beyond a fairy tale," said winger Steve Coppell when describing what it was like to play at Old Trafford for the first time. "And despite winning trophies, my debut was my highlight as a United player. My heart was jumping out of my chest and I've never had another experience like it. I wasn't running; I was floating across the grass. Words do not do the experience justice; it was a drug-like euphoric trance. I've had a few operations, and it was like that little pleasant stage after the anaesthetic. Only multiplied by a hundred. To score a goal at the Stretford End, to see all those people so happy because of something you've done was truly special."

The development of the stadium continued with the cantilever stand extended around the Scoreboard goal. Save for a tiny strip of terracing at the front of the Stretford End, Old Trafford was now fully covered for the first time in its history. Along with Goodison, it was the only stadium to offer standing and seats on all four sides.

The Old Trafford I first saw in 1984 would continue to change. The main stand roof was cantilevered and the Scoreboard Paddock cut out and replaced by a Family Stand. By 1985, Old Trafford was fully cantilevered on three sides and boasted 26,000 seats, more than any other ground. The new roof allowed floodlights to be suspended from it and the old pylon floodlights, constructed in the late 50s, were dismantled in 1987.

For a brief period, United were not the best-supported team in England. In 1987-88 and 1988-89, Liverpool's crowds had overtaken United's as the average sank below 40,000. The Stretford End badly needed replacing, but United didn't have the money. When chairman Martin Edwards agreed to sell the club to Michael Knighton in 1989, he explained his reasons thus:

"The Stretford End needed rebuilding and the price would have been around £7 million. I didn't have the money. Michael Knighton arrived out of the blue and was prepared to give me £10 million, which was more than what my shares were worth. He also said that he was going to rebuild the Stretford End and would spend a further £10 million on that. It solved both my problems. And there's another thing – what if I had turned him down and it became public knowledge that I had turned down the money which would have rebuilt the Stretford End?"

Knighton did get to play keepy-uppy in front of the Stretford End, but his bid was farcical and failed. United still needed to rebuild the stadium, funds for which would come instead from the booming gates attracted by the football played by Sir Alex Ferguson's sides in the early 90s.

"We always built stands out of the profits," explains Edwards when I spoke to him in 2009. "The money that fans were paying was going back into the club." The famous Stretford End terrace was demolished in 1992 and a new stand completed the seamless bowl that had begun 30 years earlier. Seamless and stunning maybe, but all-seated capacity was limited to just 44,600, just over half that of the San Siro and Bernabéu, and a third that of Camp Nou. Old Trafford simply didn't compare with Europe's best stadiums. There were other issues. The Stretford End has long been United's vocal heartland. Now, the centre block of seating was given over to the executive fans, while the Family Stand, launched in 1985 with 2,000 seats at the other end of the stadium, had proved so successful that it was moved into an expanded section in the new Stretford End in 1993.

"I can understand why some supporters were not happy, but there would not have been a great payback on that stand if we had just put normal seats in," says

Edwards. "I accept that the atmosphere was compromised, but we had to get a balance financially. And I know it's not the popular thing to say, but I was happy when Old Trafford became all-seat. I felt that after Hillsborough, it was the safest way forward for stadiums."

The Taylor Report, which followed the Hillsborough disaster, instructed all top-flight clubs to be all-seat, and the final terrace, the Scoreboard Paddock behind the goal, was seated in 1994. In the same section, the area designated for disabled supporters behind the goal was expanded too, with Old Trafford now boasting the best facilities for people with disabilities in Britain. Unlike at other clubs, fans with disabilities and their carers didn't have to pay for tickets.

Old Trafford was full every week and ticket prices were increased significantly (between 1988 and 1993, they rose by an average of 222% more than ticket prices at any other British club). The increases were partly to offset the limited capacity and, while they were not popular with many fans, the stadium continued to be filled.

United desperately needed a bigger capacity and the same architects, now called Atherden Fuller Leng, were again consulted. The plan envisaged a £19 million, 25,300-capacity North Stand (later named the Sir

Alex Ferguson stand), the largest stand in Britain with the largest cantilevered roof in the world. The lower tiers would be exactly the same as the 1966 stand, but they were demolished and rebuilt afresh to include a new United museum, which was opened by Pele. The upper tier of the new stand was so high that signs warned fans taking the stairs about the dangers of proceeding if they had breathing difficulties or heart conditions.

United were England's dominant team of the 90s and demand for tickets grew and grew. By 1996, the stadium capacity had risen to 55,000 thanks to the North Stand, but even this mighty structure couldn't sate demand. By the time the team won the treble in 1999, further plans for expansion were already underway.

In 2000 and 2001, two stands holding 6,000 seats apiece were constructed behind both existing stands at each end of the stadium. They raised the capacity to 67,000 and they also gave the stadium a much more impressive exterior, with the club's principal offices relocated behind an impressive glass façade (and statue of Sir Matt Busby) at the East End.

Despite the increased capacity, Old Trafford sold out for almost every first team game, with United's average attendance exceeding that of their nearest rival, Newcastle United, by 16,000. Throughout this period, United's main domestic competitors on the field were Arsenal, who were limited by their 38,000 capacity at Highbury. Arsenal cited the huge gulf in capacity between Highbury and Old Trafford as the principal reason for building the new, 60,000-capacity Emirates Stadium.

The huge demand for tickets also affected the demographics of the stadium. In the past, certain stands had attracted different types of supporters. Younger, more boisterous Reds frequented the Stretford End or the United Road terrace to be close to the away fans, who stood behind the goal in the Scoreboard Paddock. For the same reason, K-Stand behind the goal became a popular place to sit in the late 1980s. A friendly rivalry developed with J-Stand next door, a 1,600 segment of seating. You didn't sit in the two stands along the side of the pitch if you wanted to sing. No, they were for those who wanted to study the game and dissect tactics.

Now, the boundaries are more blurred. Sure, executive supporters don't walk around the ground wearing jesters' hats and waving scarves, but different types of fans are spread around the stadium. Because season tickets were so hard to come by for much of the 1990s, fans didn't really have a choice where they sat, and so took whatever was offered.

One of the reasons the Glazers (and before them Murdoch) were so keen to buy United was because of the consistently phenomenal support enjoyed by the club. They had been in charge for one year when two new quadrant sections were opened in 2006. These sections linked the upper tiers and provided a bowl effect on three sides of the ground. They each held 8,000 seats, including significant executive facilities, and boosted the capacity to 76,000. And still Old Trafford was full.

The new increased capacity allowed United to become the most supported team in European football several times between 2006 and 2012, edging ahead of Barcelona, Real Madrid and Borussia Dortmund. United filled the stadium despite increasing the ticket prices by up to 30% in the first four years of the Glazers. An economic downturn meant demand lessened, and prices were all but held from 2010 onwards.

The developments at the stadium weren't just limited to increasing the capacity. The club bought huge swathes of land around the ground since 1994, turning it into car parks. That land has increased in value as the neighbouring Salford Quays has boomed.

Few rival clubs have the luxury of spare land around their homes like United. Liverpool, Chelsea, Tottenham and Everton are all hamstrung by a lack of space, yet it's a lack of space on one side of Old Trafford that is the one obstacle to future development.

Future expansion of Old Trafford is possible, but any extra seating would have to be above the single-tiered main stand, now dwarfed by its neighbours. The main Manchester to Liverpool rail line runs behind the stand, with housing directly behind that. Another tier of seating, which would boost capacity to as high as 97,000, is possible, but it would be far more costly than any developments seen before. It may happen, but not in a challenging economic climate.

As it stands, Old Trafford is a vast cavity of redness. Red always looks better than blue in stadiums, more passionate: warm. United's home for more than a century may be derided for its fading atmosphere, but on its day (or night) for a big European game or a match against Liverpool or City, it's still a sight to behold, just as it was on that first visit.

Andy Mitten – whose great-uncle Charlie Mitten starred in Matt Busby's first great side – started the Manchester United fanzine *United We Stand* in 1989, when he was aged 15; he continues to edit the publication and writes in each issue. He has written 11 books, including the critically acclaimed *We're the Famous Man United*, Paddy Crerand's autobiography *Never Turn The Other Cheek* and *Mad For It – From Blackpool to Barcelona, Football's Greatest Rivalries*.

THIRTEEN

ROY
BY MARK KELLEHER

THE CHANCES OF MANCHESTER United's most deco-
rated captain in its history, Roy Maurice Keane, ever
having a statue erected in his honour on the forecourt
just outside Old Trafford are tellingly slim. There
will be no room alongside the holy trinity of Charlton, Edwards and Law for a man so disgusted by the
thought of failure that limbs regularly went on the
line to secure victory. The devastating duo of Giggs
and Scholes, if they ever retire, will one day have their
effigies carved into bronzed steel, permanent remind-
ers of their incomparable legacies, and places to go for

fathers to remember and tell their sons of glories past. Enshrined in the club's enormous history, they will be the figureheads most likely looked upon as the names that encompassed a rich period of success. It is unlikely that any club could ever mirror such a spell again.

Keane's absence, however, will have little to do with a playing career that spanned 12 years of consistent excellence and unbridled success, both as an individual and as the lieutenant general of United's greatest ever side. Despite spearheading United into a rare uncharted territory, the snarling Corkonian will also be remembered for his odd individualism, an edge that ensured any standard that dropped below his own was to be lamented and cursed at.

While those with a predilection for red will have the near-dictatorial performances, the dominating master classes and on-pitch wars embedded into their minds, the rest will remember the traits that separated him from anyone else who has ever played the game. The maniacal eyes, the borderline-sociopathic view of life outside the game, and his mistrust of football and its characters, all have led to Keane's title of enigma. In an almost cruel twist of fate, his obsessive demand for standards, which were at times unreachable, ensured that the strengths that had served to bring him to the very top also became weaknesses in his later career. In a career of immense victories and spiralling controversies, what Keane lacked in flair and skill, he made up for in function and a soldier-like philosophy towards the game. Those with him, wounded or otherwise, he would carry – those on the other side of the battlefield he would destroy. He was never the most technically gifted player, but United are unlikely to ever have one as interesting or as hell-bent on success. Part of the reason why he'll never have a statue is because he won't want one. Keane was the most perfect of team-men, because – ironically – he was an individual.

His story has filled acres of column space and tomes, detailed documentations all chasing answers: who was he then, who is he now and why did he become such an intriguing character? From the cut-up turf throughout Cork City, where a diminutive young Keane honed his trade, to St Colman's Park in Cobh, where he attracted a chasing pack of scouts, Ireland's most famous son has left behind a trail of anecdotes, early glories and myths. While wider Ireland is notoriously known as an island of "begrudgers," the loyalty Keane is met with on Leeside is akin to the type of ceaseless devotion that the most fundamental of believers extend towards their Gods. If United were already adored in Cork before his move, his signing for them in the summer of 1993 helped spread a new wave of red throughout the county.

Keane first came to prominence under the gaze of Brian Clough at Nottingham Forest, but it was his move to Lancashire that helped the trajectory of a career that would always centre on winning. A British transfer record at the time, the now minimal sum of £3.75 million changed hands, and one of the first steps towards a prolonged period of success was put in place for both individual and club. Assuming the burden of midfield leader from the waning Bryan Robson, Keane – as he would so often later do – used pressure as the fuel to ignite his and his teammates' excellence.

Within three years he had won two doubles, unprecedented success for a club that would drive on towards further surreal highs. Having attained captaincy following Eric Cantona's untimely retirement, Keane's career was soon cast into doubt as he lay upended at Elland Road, his cruciate ligament severely damaged. He was to spend eight months sidelined, while Arsenal pilfered what looked destined to be United's title. If the sight of Keane in agony, with Alf-Inge Haaland standing over him and roaring at him to get up and stop faking it, was to bring further significance four years later, it was perhaps Keane's recovery – and what soon followed – that encompassed all that he brought to the club and what the club brought to him.

Those who love football do so for its incomparable beauty, first and foremost; for the gazelle-like glide that propels wingers; for the thunderous 30-yard strike that hits the top corner; for the giant-slaying and drama that resides in no other sport. No team will ever have a season quite like United's 1999 campaign. It was a season that perfectly captured the style, the heart and the hunger, woven into United's fabric. Step aside from the magnificence of its end, the wealth of comebacks, last-minute dramas and powerful team displays, and you'll see a season so dreamlike it would embarrass even the most imaginative of fantasy-fiction writers. And even though the most magical of its moments will forever be associated with Solskjaer and Sheringham, puppet master Keane's influence was pivotal.

While some aspects of 1999 may fade from memory, any Red of the right age will remember the overall brilliance of that particular campaign. From the worrying lows of early season, to the breathtaking aesthetics in the late hours in Camp Nou, it was a feat that couldn't be repeated again. In classic United style, where fluidity takes precedence over function, leaked goals were counterbalanced by the scoring of many more. It was a season packed with epic games and memorable thrillers. Both 3-3 draws with Barcelona in the European Cup group stages were early hints of what was to come.

There was the 8-1 annihilation of Nottingham Forest, a 90-minute showcase of United's relentless front line. They went unbeaten from December, and secured the league on the final day when Andy Cole's lob against Spurs put paid to Arsenal's hopes of retaining the title. But it was in cup competitions that United soared to new heights, led by the ruthless Keane. Stationed in the infamous, 'Group of Death' alongside the domineering Bayern Munich and Barcelona, as well as Danish side Brondby, United's path to glory looked ominous. History ensures that all memory of the club's trail to success appears rosy, but little thought is given to the anxiety the group provided. Having battled to four draws and two wins, United left the group as runners-up, beating the Catalans by two points.

If Keane's total influence was to come later, it was to be found too in the group stage. Already a scorer against Brondby, it was Keane's critical opener against Munich that led United to Italy for a quarter-final joust with Inter Milan. It was in the next stage, however, that Keane put in his most memorable performance in a United shirt – a performance of such absolute selflessness and dominance even his (and the club's) most ardent haters stood wide-eyed in awe. A late equaliser had cemented a tight 1-1 draw at home to Juventus in the first leg. Just 10 minutes into the second, Juventus led 2-0 on the night, 3-1 on aggregate. Despite the calamitous start, it was to be another night of highs.

Up against the brilliance of Zidane and Deschamps, Keane excelled, raised a dismayed United team, and headed a collective of warriors intent on securing unlikely victory. His expertly-timed header proffered the first moment of hope, the trigger United needed to regain a foothold in the match. It wasn't for style alone that Keane's performance is held as remarkable. A foul on Zidane earned him a harsh booking and a subsequent suspension from the final that followed. As the card was held aloft, Keane knew its repercussions. But he was a professional to the end, one of those limited few who played with heart, mindful of those suffering in the stands. Shirking responsibility, knowing he would miss club football's grandest stage, would have been the easy thing to do. Keane didn't do easy. He was, and still is, tortured by defeat. Yorke and Cole may have turned the game in United's favour, but it was Keane who inspired victory on one of the club's finest nights. It defined Keane's ingrained approach and inspired Sir

Alex Ferguson to offer one of his most memorable quotes: "It was the most emphatic display of selflessness I have seen on a football field. Pounding over every blade of grass, competing as if he would rather die of exhaustion than lose, he inspired all around him. I felt it was an honour to be associated with such a player."

Keane's medal haul would grow over the next six years, as he led United to three more titles and an FA Cup. In 2000, his value to the wider game was recognised when he snared both the Football Writers' Association Footballer of the Year and PFA Players' Player of the Year awards. Even with a swathe of medals and accolades under his belt, Keane's form rarely fluctuated. The aggression, the unerring will to win and his sheer determination were to remain ceaseless. The controversies also continued to shadow him – on and off the field dramas that Keane himself often appeared to activate. With Roy, the media had a plaything, one who was to be listened to when speaking. Keane abhors the cliché, the empty gestures uttered by empty-headed footballers who are well trained in the art of on-air tedium. In 2001, a demonic Keane took vengeance on the aforementioned Alf Inge Haaland, catching him high on the leg with a wild stamp. The premeditated act was later outlined in Keane's controversial autobiography, *Keane: The Autobiography*, a colourful tirade that would later earn him a heavy fine and ban. A year later, the ever-divisive Keane drew a battle line through Ireland from Saipan, the scene of perhaps his most historic tussle. Having become entangled with Mick McCarthy and senior staff over training conditions, the furore grew and Keane – embroiled in a verbal joust with his manager – refused to play any further part in Ireland's World Cup campaign.

Across the nation arguments ensued. On one side, Keane was considered a treacherous thug who had let himself and his country down. On the other, specifically in his hometown, his displeasure with poor standards was the mark of a consummate professional. The turmoil, it would later turn out, would be the first of two off-field misdemeanours that cast shadows over what was a largely pristine career. Three years after the incident, Keane came to loggerheads with a man who is rarely beaten. His criticism of his underperforming teammates on the club's in-house television station was to be the sad harbinger of destruction for his ·United career.

As shown with the 2003 flogging of David Beckham, Ferguson isn't one for forgiveness. Any disturbance of his dictatorial command is eradicated.

The identity of the assailant matters little. Power, it is clear, rests in the hands of the manager and in his alone. On reflection, the relationship between Keane and Ferguson was always likely to lead to a catastrophic end. The traits that so handsomely bound them together – unending drive, a fiery desire to win, a hatred of failure – were also the sort that would tear them apart. It was poetic, almost, that it wasn't to end with a handshake, a photo finish and an aged Keane playing out to rapturous cheers in a last appearance. One day he was there, club captain and fearsome leader, the next his locker was empty. No goodbyes. The end had arrived. United and he would go their separate ways. For the fans, it was a sad conclusion. But it was also a natural one.

Seven years on from his departure, Keane's name still occasionally reverberates around Old Trafford to the tune of 'Hey Jude'. He is remembered for what he brought, but deep within the supporters' psyche he is also remembered because he is missed. United have achieved further success in the wake of his departure, but the void left since his leaving remains unfilled. The possibility of discovering a player in the same mould is near impossible. One to replace his ability, yes, but a combatant with the same mental make-up is unlikely to appear again. Few recall all of Keane's 33 goals for United. He was about more than what he did with the ball. When Keane delves into memory now, partaking in the excruciating task of having to discuss his past genius, he speaks with a predictable modesty. He was merely part of a vast and well-oiled machine, he will decree. Observers will note that he was the engine.

He hasn't always been the most likeable of men. Utterances to the press often carry an agenda, a tinge of bitterness left over from wounds that never healed. His honesty, something few players show in today's false climate, was and still is searing. In a club career that spanned seventeen years and four clubs, as well as an international career that saw him earn 67 caps, few friends from the game remain.

It is back to Rockmount, the club where it all began, that he returns, to those whom he can trust, modest folk with whom he first stepped onto a pitch. He is well travelled, and still resides in England, but that unique Corkonian spirit courses through his veins. It is a will to do better than those around you and to achieve what to others may seem improbable. Keane's story is a complex one, a narrative with many peaks and some troughs. He is unquestionably one of the most intriguing characters to have ever kicked a football.

Mark Kelleher lives in Cork. His writing features regularly in the *Evening Echo* and on the *Huffington Post UK* and stretford-end.com. Disillusioned with the Glazer regime and modern football's direction, he yearns for the blissful ignorance that steered his childhood adoration for the game.

FOURTEEN

A UNITED IRELAND
BY MIGUEL DELANEY

As THE BUSBY BABES began to capture the imagination of the continent in the mid-1950s, an intriguing idea spread among the English press. What the young Manchester United side was doing, after all, was more or less unprecedented in what was a difficult decade for the country's football. Not only were they displaying an admirable cohesion unseen in England since the visit of Hungary in 1953, they were enjoying success on the international front that was in stark contrast to the national team at the time. As such, it was argued that the entire England first

XI for the 1958 World Cup should be drawn from Old Trafford.

There was, however, one significant problem with that proposal. As the celebrated football journalist Henry Rose wrote in the *Daily Express*, it simply wouldn't have the same effect. The reason: at United "their main cog is an Irishman". Even though that was to become something of a theme at Old Trafford, Liam Whelan's influence ultimately went way beyond the pitch. According to many, he was one of the most innately talented of the Babes. A playmaking and prolific inside forward, Whelan was the player Bobby Charlton looked up to most after Duncan Edwards.

"I always wanted to be the best in the world," Charlton once said, "but knew I wouldn't be as long as Billy Whelan was around."

Indeed, when the renowned Real Madrid side finally ended United's first tilt at the European Cup in the 1956-57 semi-finals, Matt Busby wasn't too worried. Gesturing towards Charlton and Whelan, he said: "I've got these two and they're going to be as good as [Ferenc] Puskas and [Alfredo] Di Stefano."

Sadly, Busby would never get to see the two play together in their prime. United's next European campaign didn't end in triumph but in tragedy. On 6 February 1958, the club's Elizabethan aircraft failed in its second attempt to take off from the ice-covered Munich runway and 23 people lost their lives. Eight of the departed were players in Busby's brilliant young side. And, of those, all were English except one: Whelan. The Munich air disaster was the moment in which the club colour black took on a very different meaning for United, but a tinge of green should perhaps have been added too. It was also the moment in which a genuine emotional depth was added to the club's already rich relationship with Ireland.

As a result of the pride that the quiet and humble Whelan brought his country, his funeral procession was reported to have been the third largest ever seen in Dublin's Glasnevin cemetery up to that time; only the numbers attending the funerals of the leaders of the 1916 Rising and War of Independence hero Michael Collins were higher.

"From the airport down, there were people at the side of the road all the way until we came to Whitehall, where the big church is," Whelan's brother Christy says. "From there, it was thronged on each side of the road. It was packed all the way up Dorset Street, Drumcondra Road, packed all the way to the graveyard."

For the thousands present, it was impossible not to feel a connection to United from that point on. But, while the occasion undoubtedly forged an association that would be passed on to subsequent generations, it also cemented an already well-established relationship.

Even before the Munich air disaster, United's links with Ireland ran deeper and wider than did the links between Ireland and any other club in England. For a start, United were the first English side to sign an Irish football professional. John Peden, who was bought from Linfield in 1893, was the first of 65 internationals from Ireland and Northern Ireland to play for the club: 31 of these internationals were from Northern Ireland, 34 from the Republic. As it stands, United have featured more Irish internationals than have any other football club outside the island of Ireland.

In the case of the Republic, for example, only Shamrock Rovers (82 players), Shelbourne (51), Bohemians (49) and Dundalk (38) have supplied more. Next on the list after United's quota of 34 players from the Republic is Whelan's first club, Home Farm, which has had 33 Irish internationals, followed by Sunderland, which has had 28 Irish players.

It isn't just the number of caps, however, but the nature of them. In 1965, United youth graduate Shay Brennan became the first player born outside Ireland to represent the country. A second-generation migrant, he qualified through the so-called 'Granny rule', which Jack Charlton would so exploit in later years. That, however, has always been something of an unfair misnomer. Throughout the last few decades, Article 18 of FIFA's rules on nationality and eligibility merely read: "Any person who is a naturalised citizen of a country by virtue of that country's laws shall be eligible to play for a national or representative team of that country." Unlike most citizenship laws, however, Ireland's laws entitle anyone whose grandparent was an Irish citizen to be granted an Irish passport, thus correctly reflecting the country's history of emigration. And few cities in the world represent that history of emigration better than Manchester.

Naturally, such deep links between club and country can be attributed to much more than mere football. At present, the annual Manchester Irish Festival is the largest in the United Kingdom and one of the biggest in the world. Up to a third of the city's population is estimated to be of Irish descent, and this background is evident in the names of some of the city's most famous modern cultural figures: Morrissey, the Gallagher brothers, Steve Coogan. As such, the Irish connection among the club's support didn't so much straddle the Irish Sea as straddle entire families. That, of course, is a consequence of a rich past.

Due to its location and size, Manchester bore the brunt of the first significant waves of Irish emigration in the early part of the 19th century. By 1841, as the ruinous conditions which led to the devastating Irish famine escalated, a tenth of the city's entire population was Irish. The overwhelming majority, meanwhile, were living in squalor. So extensive was the poverty, in fact, that the sociologist Frederich Engels even made the 'Little Ireland' slum in the Ancoats area of the city a subject of his 1845 book *The Condition of the Working Class in England*.

"The New Town, known also as Irish Town, stretches up a hill of clay, beyond the Old Town, between the Irk and St George's Road. Here, all the features of a city are lost. Single rows of houses or groups of streets stand, here and there, like little villages on the naked, not even grass-grown clay soil; the houses, or rather cottages, are in bad order, never repaired, filthy, with damp, unclean, cellar dwellings; the lanes are neither paved nor supplied with sewers, but harbour numerous colonies of swine penned in small sties or yards, or wandering unrestrained through the neighbourhood."

Engels even went so far as to provide a description of what was supposedly a typical Irishman in Manchester at the time.

"He builds a pigsty against the house wall as he did at home and if he is prevented from doing this, he lets the pig sleep in the room with himself. The Irishman loves his pig as the Arab his horse, with the difference that he sells it when it is fat enough to kill. Otherwise, he eats and sleeps with it, his children play with it, ride upon it, roll in the dirt with it, as anyone may see a thousand times repeated in all the great towns of England."

The dwellers of such conditions were naturally prepared to take whatever work came their way, even if it meant accepting lower pay than that offered to locals. This inevitably led to tension, especially when Irish workers were brought in to break strikes.

Not surprisingly, such poverty also provided the breeding ground for revolution. Manchester was the location of one of the trigger moments in the history of the Irish nationalist movement. In 1867, as plans for an armed uprising against British rule in Ireland grew, two members of the Fenian Brotherhood were arrested in the city for "behaving suspiciously in a doorway". Later, as they were being transported from court to prison, their carriage was ambushed by 30 Fenians, and one policeman was shot. While the two leaders of the Fenian Brotherhood managed to escape, three of the ambushers did not; they were subsequently charged with murder and executed. The three: William Philip Allen, Michael Larkin and Michael O'Brien would go down in history as the 'Manchester Martyrs'.

During the 11 short years between the violent events of 1867 and 1878 (when the Newton Heath Lancashire and Yorkshire Railway Club was founded), the Irish community became increasingly integrated into Manchester society; so much so that in 1902, when the decision was made to change the name of the club (a move designed to signal a fresh start after a series of financial difficulties), they were only a few votes shy of the number required to rename it Manchester Celtic.

The institution that was to become known as Manchester United already had a reputation for engendering deep support among the Irish migrant community. On the Bank Street terraces, the common bond helped to break down divisions between disparate communities while, on the pitch, such integration was further exemplified by players bearing names like Moore and Kennedy. However, while United's early teams featured distinguished figures such as future Barcelona manager Patrick O'Connell, it wasn't until the 1930s that the club would fully tap into its rich seam of talented Irish players. Ironically, that was all down to one seemingly unremarkable individual, Billy Behan, a goalkeeper who made just one first team appearance for Manchester United, and that was in the 1933-34 season, a period when the club was languishing in the second division.

While Behan could never have been described as anything more than third-choice goalkeeper, his true talents lay in other areas, and his eventual transfer back to Shelbourne in 1934 was to prove one of the most profitable in United's history. From there, he became the club's main scout in Ireland. As John Giles later put it, Behan "had a kind of sixth sense for identifying the players who would make it, a bit like the way that, say, Vincent O'Brien could look at a yearling and, in his mind's eye, see a Derby winner. At United, they valued their Irish links, not least because of the calibre of player that Billy Behan had found for them."

Behan proved that almost straight away. One of the first players he identified, in 1936, Johnny Carey, became one of the most famous and forceful figures in the club's history. Carey, who made his debut at the start of the 1937-38 season at the age of 18, went on to help United secure promotion to the First Division after a seven-year absence.

Almost immediately, Carey's life and career were interrupted by the outbreak of the Second World War. By the time the war ended six years later, however,

Carey was deemed sufficiently mature to assume responsibility for captaining the first great side to be created by new United manager Matt Busby, himself of Irish descent and a devout Catholic. In so many senses, a legend was born.

Carey's involvement in Manchester United succeeded in generating greater awareness of the club back in Ireland. Even though the early 50s in Ireland were not characterised by widespread media coverage of English football matches, or travel from Ireland to see those matches, the young Johnny Giles was already referring to United as "my team". Many others in Ireland were starting to do the same. The subsequent arrival of Liam Whelan on the scene further altered this dynamic forever. Whelan's brother Christy tells the story of how the club, somewhat fortuitously, came to sign the Irish Babe.

"By 14, at Home Farm, [Liam] was already doing all the dribbling he was famous for. He used to have two players marking him then, but it didn't always work. Though United's scout Billy Behan had been watching him, no one made an approach, not even the League of Ireland clubs. Now, I used to be always complaining to my mother, 'there's something wrong here because he's the best player in this country' and she used to say 'ah, it's because you're his brother'. But it wasn't. Then, when he was 17, Behan and Bert Whalley [United's coach] were over to watch a lad named Vinnie Ryan play for Home Farm and Liam played a blinder. Bert Whalley said to Billy, 'forget about Vinnie Ryan for the moment, get that lad Whelan, we want him immediately.' Later that night, I was in bed and Liam came to shake me awake. He said 'there's a man here from Manchester United', and I responded: 'It's about bloody time!'"

On arriving at Old Trafford, Whelan was given one piece of advice from the old legend Carey: "Hold on to your given name as long as you can because, for sure, they will be calling you something else soon."

Inevitably, just as Jackie Carey became Johnny once he was established in England, Liam became Billy. Meanwhile, Giles had gone from being called John to being called Johnny. In his autobiography, *John Giles: A Football Man – My Autobiography*, he recounts a journey that would become common for so many young Irish players.

"I was not flying to Manchester on a first-class ticket with Aer Lingus, accompanied by my parents and my agent... it was 1955, and I went over on the boat, on my own. I arrived in Liverpool early in the morning, and then I got the train from Liverpool to Manchester, on my own. Joe Armstrong [the United chief scout] was waiting for me at Manchester Central

Station. So, amid all the excitement, I had worries too; about getting lost, or getting on the wrong train in Liverpool, or otherwise seeing my dream getting away from me through some mad misfortune."

Difficulties were illustrated in other ways, not least when the dreadful news from Munich began to filter through. The most tragic aspect of all, however, was that Liam Whelan wasn't even meant to be on the flight. Although he was out injured for the second leg of Manchester United's 1957-58 European Cup quarter-final against Red Star Belgrade, he had decided to travel with the team nonetheless.

"You don't hold any animosity or anything like that," Christy Whelan says. "It's just how it works out. I remember everything vividly, all the faces and especially – the hardest part – what my mother went through. I was working in Dublin Corporation, but was on strike, so I was at home on the sixth. My mother was out the back ironing with my sister when I saw Charlie Jackson, from Home Farm, coming up. He worked in the Guinness Brewery and he was in his work clothes. It was only my mother that twigged that. She turned around and said 'Charlie, is there something wrong?' and he said 'Did you not hear anything?' Now, we used to have a sideboard with all Liam's trophies on it, with a clock, and he would always tell my mother what time he'd be flying home at. She pointed to it and said 'the clock, they're home Charlie.'

'I'm afraid not Mrs Whelan.'

Typically, the club would be rebuilt with an Irish core. Shay Brennan started and scored in the emotional first game after the Munich air disaster, a 3-0 FA Cup win over Sheffield Wednesday. Soon, Giles and Joe Carolan would also join up with the first team. Within two years, Noel Cantwell had signed for the club. Within 10 years, Brennan and Tony Dunne would form the full-back duo in the United team that finally won the European Cup.

Dunne was only one of the stars who had been discovered by Behan; his other discoveries included the likes of Don Givens, Mick Martin, Gerry Daly and Kevin Moran.

Behan's involvement with United, coupled with the effects of numerous Irish community-related links, created a unique legacy. It was responsible for the emergence of a large number of Irish players and, more importantly, quality players.

Another remarkable aspect of United's connection with Ireland is that, from Carey to Roy Keane, the club enjoyed a virtually unbroken line of the very best talent. Virtually every Irish footballer who has come anywhere close to being considered 'world class' has played at Old

Trafford. After Carey, Whelan and Giles came the force of Frank Stapleton, the precision of Paul McGrath, the assurance of Denis Irwin, and the drive of Roy Keane. The only true exceptions have been Liam Brady, who grew up a United supporter but ended up at Arsenal and, to a lesser extent, Ronnie Whelan. None of those names, however, could come close to the talent of an Irishman from a very different background: George Best.

If the Busby Babes added an emotional depth to Irish support for Manchester United, Best provided the energy, the romance and the glamour. At a time when television and *Match of the Day* were already drastically changing the country's consumption of football, moving it further away from the modesty of the domestic league, the sport's first superstar brought box-office brilliance.

That, however, is perhaps one of the more interesting and underappreciated aspects of the winger's career at United. At the precise period when the situation in Best's native Northern Ireland was escalating and nearing the point that would trigger the Troubles, he wasn't actually perceived by the majority of southern fans as a Belfast Protestant, or indeed as in any way political or separate. Instead, he was simply seen as distinct in another, much more positive way: the star, the talent, the icon, the best.

While Best's ability and personality allowed him to transcend the Troubles, equally, it cannot be denied that he merely reflected the general history of Northern Irish players at Old Trafford. Despite the context of something as serious as the political situation in Ulster, United once again served to make barriers and divisions seem irrelevant.

Consider, for example, the case of the outside right, Thomas Morrison, who played for Glasgow Celtic. Morrison was from a Protestant background, but despite Glasgow Celtic's clear association with the Catholic side of the divide, he actually became the first Irish native to play for the club in 1895, eventually joining Manchester United seven years later.

Almost a decade after that, Belfast-born Mickey Hamill was the only Irish presence at the club during their first ever trophy-winning spell of two leagues and one FA Cup, between 1908 and 1911. He would later refuse to play for the Irish national team, which wouldn't split into two until after the political partition of 1921, due to the perceived discrimination against Catholic players at the time.

At Old Trafford, of course, there was no divide. Moreover, if the majority of the Republic's greatest ever players lined out for United, so too did Northern Ireland's. Before Best, there was Jackie Blanchflower.

The brother of Tottenham's Danny, his career was ended by the injuries suffered in the Munich air disaster. Blanchflower's fate might have been worse, however, had he not been pulled from the wreckage by 'The Hero of Munich', Magherafelt-born Harry Gregg.

After Best came Sammy McIlroy, Jimmy Nichol and the match winner of the 1985 FA Cup final, Norman Whiteside. Today, players like Johnny Evans and Robbie Brady continue to carry the torch. Fuelled by family connections, a deep history and the most renowned players, the number of Irish fans visiting Old Trafford every year is higher than the number of Irish fans visiting any other football stadium in the world.

Whatever about a united Ireland, it seems the island will always be some way United.

___

Miguel Delaney is a football writer for ESPN, the *Irish Examiner*, *The Independent* and the *Evening Herald*. He was nominated for Irish Sports Journalist of the Year in 2011 and is the author of *Stuttgart to Saipan*, which was published in 2010. He is based in London.

FIFTEEN

THE NOSEY NEIGHBOURS
BY LUCIA ZANETTI

I'VE GOT AN AWFUL memory, there's no getting away from it. I can't remember what I had for tea last night, so I'm damned if I can refer to my childhood in a neat, chronologically coherent way. Neighbours, mates, school – they blur into one and I often find myself trying to remember the names of kids I grew up with for years, with fruitless results. So, in football, where fandom is a massive cock-measuring competition, to be encyclopaedic about dates and match results is seen as the litmus test for your 'proper' fan, the years can seem to merge into one.

But there is one football date I can bring to mind with such startling clarity. So much so that even now as I write I am transported back to that time, that day, that *child*...

It was a boiling hot Monday morning, three weeks into the new school year. We were Top Juniors, the oldest pupils in the school, and high on potentially powerful possibilities. Manchester City Council – a Labour council – had ignored the 'recommendations' of Thatcher some years previously, and so everyone in our class had their own tiny bottle of whole milk pierced with a thin, blue straw. They were supped first thing, before being left lingering in their crate at the doorway; the heat of the classroom warming them, leaving us engulfed in an acrid, sour fug.

I was forced to sit at the desk directly in front of our teacher, next to a kid called Michael Beech. Michael had a permanent trail of neon snot running from his nose to his mouth. Occasionally, his tongue would dart out to mop up the nasal nectar, rendering his upper lip chapped, red and flaky. Needless to say, I couldn't even *look* at him. Because he sat on my right, my neck was permanently swivelled to the left, facing the wall-length row of windows in our prefabricated classroom extension of the main school. It was as my face was contorted thus that I first saw him.

Damien Costello. Damien *Twatting* Costello.

The first thing I noticed about Damien was his shiny, bowl-shaped haircut. You have to remember that this was 1989, and Manchester was on the precipice of becoming the cultural capital of the world. I don't mean like the Scouse 'Capital of Culture', with its roots in the decades-old legacy of ONE band. I mean tangible, bona fide, and *proper*.

That year heralded the debut albums of The Stone Roses, De La Soul, and Soul II Soul. Earlier still, we'd had the music of The Smiths, New Order, and Joy Division, and the emergence of new bands like Happy Mondays and Inspiral Carpets. Our city was also the pioneering hub of electronic music, and the Haçienda was set to become (as reported by US *Newsweek)* "… the most famous nightclub in the world."

No Mancunians were impervious to Manchester's cultural significance, and given that there was no uniform in our school, it was commonplace to see iconic Smiths, Stone Roses, and Happy Mondays T-shirts in the playground, along with rows of bowl haircuts, bell-bottom jeans and Clarks Wallabees.

After the hair, the second thing I noticed about Damien was his massive grin. His cheeks obscured his eye sockets and there were two rows of teeth on display. You'd be forgiven for overlooking that broad grin, given that it was a beautiful, late-summer morning and he was a young child enjoying his final year at primary school. Why *wouldn't* his smile match that of Little Orphan Annie on adoption day? Maybe because it was the only smile Damien Costello had ever exhibited in our previous six years of shared schooling. So unacquainted with the smile was he, that the very sight of him smiling was a tremendous shock. Before I'd had time to register the smile's intent, its very existence served to shake me to my foundations.

It was then that I noticed the third thing. He was wearing a bright, white T-shirt, on the front of which was a massive cartoon bulldog and a colour print of Manchester City Football Club's emblem. As he turned the corner and the back of his shiny, bowl-head hair bobbed and glistened in the morning sun, I saw what was written on the back:

Manchester City   5   v   1   Manchester United
September 23rd 1989

This was less than *two days* after the football match. When you take into account that one of those days was a Sunday – The *Lord's* Day – in an era before supermarket Sunday opening, and when *everything* was shut, it was an impressively swift response to a non-crucial match result by Manchester City and indicative of what United fans in Manchester have endured whenever City have historically made their two-game-a-season monumental effort to defeat us.

The match itself had been pretty catastrophic, especially considering that Michael Knighton had recently forked out for the League's most expensive ever player – Gary Pallister – who'd made some appalling errors during the game, clearly (given that he was a defender and we'd conceded *five* goals). It's been well documented as the trigger for the darkest time in Ferguson's career, with many fans and journalists calling for his head on a platter. Knighton's spending spree particularly disturbed the MCFC support and they positioned themselves as the dam, standing against big money in football, an argument they returned to on countless occasions in the ensuing years, during our Golden era. Chants of "Fergie out!" came not only from our fans, but also from The Blues in an attempt to wind things up and revel in our defeat.

And revelling in the rare and fleeting defeats of Manchester United during the last 25 years or so has, to me, come to represent City fans. Extracting joy, not from their own lacklustre performances, but from the minute mishaps of their infinitely more successful and talented neighbours. Not so much the Fergie- dubbed

"Noisy Neighbours", as (recurring haemorrhoid-style) *Nosey* Neighbours, with their, "How can they afford that car?" "They get more wheelie bins than us", "Have you seen the state of their hedges?" sort of mentality.

Manchester City aren't our greatest rivals, not even nearly. Liverpool are our greatest rivals, just as we are theirs. The fact is that up until very recently Manchester City hadn't even *been* our rivals in any footballing sense. City are small time regardless of their footballing achievements, because they are trapped in a cycle of measuring themselves against us. It's like driving a Ferrari with the sole intention of showing off to your ex-boss. You never just get to enjoy driving the car.

This is not to say that we don't enjoy beating Manchester City, because we do. But the main reason we like beating City is not due to any real sense of occasion, or meeting of minds. Rather, the reason is to save ourselves from days, months, or, in some cases, *years* of sanctimonious and ridiculously disproportionate gloating.

There's no denying that it's a joyous thing to be armed with success when snaking your way to work, college, or school on a Monday morning, knowing you'll face plenty of "the enemy." But there's wanting to beat the other team and glean joy from the victory, and then there's keeping hold of the memorabilia from a football match at the start of a season where your team (much like the next nearly quarter-century) won precisely *fuck all*.

To put that into some sort of perspective, 1989-90 saw both Manchester United and City finish the season languishing in the lower half of the league table, although United finished a spot higher on goal difference. The same season saw United's first silverware under Ferguson when we won the FA Cup against Crystal Palace in the replay. Yet, The Bitters cling on to that irrelevant result at the start of a disappointing season like it was the last purple toffee in the tin.

The problem is that while we went on to enjoy our most successful footballing period, garnering new rivalries and enjoying an unrivalled perspective, City have focused on our success to their detriment. If a decision goes United's way, it's because the ref's on the payroll. As Ferguson inferred, they've spent decades watching their own matches with one ear to the radio, listening in on our game regardless of the impact on their own.

Which brings us to the second salient fact about Manchester City and their support.

During Manchester United's reign as the dominant team in English football, it served the media well to construct the idea of our fans as transient, and in pursuit only of the glory of their team's success. The accuracy of whether or not new lightweight fans were acquired is too tedious for me to give much attention to. The answer is of course, yes, but any sporting success brings with it new fans, and those sort of fans were wearing Liverpool shirts in the 80s, and are wearing City shirts now. It's the nature of the game, the nature of support and makes very little difference to long-term fans other than profit, which (in *some* cases) makes for the acquisition of better players. However, something that is rarely factored into the concept of the 'glory hunt' is the opposing notion: that of nobility in failure. The gravitas one acquires by supporting a team that relentlessly fails is seen by many as a badge of honour. I am fortunate in that my football team has enjoyed massive success for most of my adult life, but in another sense my mettle has not been tested.

City fans – perversely – have enjoyed their unwarranted reputation as Manchester's gallant losers. They have relished in their status, not as winners, but as our poorly-treated neighbours. There are very few lengths a City fan won't go to, for example, to explain how they are the *true* Mancunian team. United fans don't have that same inclination.

If we had the mindset of City fans, we'd take great delight in telling you that despite the current location of Old Trafford, we were formed in Clayton – well within the boundaries of Manchester proper – several years *before* Manchester City. We'd go on to explain that the city's main newspaper, the *Manchester Evening News* (sometimes dubbed *Manchester Evening Blues* by Mancunian Reds, for its commitment to Manchester City column inches) has conducted numerous surveys proving conclusively that there are significantly more Manchester United than Manchester City fans living in Manchester. *Significantly* more. Rendering the classic "You're from Manchester and support *United*? No way!" as inaccurate as it is unfunny. But United fans aren't really that arsed. The whining pedantry about the significance of the borders of Manchester have never held the same resonance for us, because a) our team win and b) every United fan knows – regardless of surveys – that Manchester is red.

But while we're on the topic of what isn't funny, there's a media-constructed myth about City fans having a great sense of humour. The irony of which is *hilarious*. I won't allow my own bias to cloud this misconception further by pointing out that both Bernard Manning and the Gallagher brothers are Mancunian City fans and Steve Coogan and the late Tony Wilson are/were Mancunian Reds. Listing celebrity allegiances is as dull to read as it is to acquire, and Lord *knows* United have our fair share of celebrity fan knobheads, so allow me to demonstrate the wit of the Manchester City support using tangible examples of behaviour.

It will take monumental effort to try to explain the subtle complexity of the comedic reasoning behind City's inflatables era, but allow me to try. It was 1987 and City acquired a new striker, Imre Varadi. He never made much of an impact at any of the numerous clubs he played for, and never stayed anywhere longer than two years. You might remember him playing briefly for Leeds United (alongside The King) and helping them secure the final First Division League Title in 1992. But probably not, because he hadn't played the requisite number of games for them that season (three) to even secure a winner's medal. Anyway, legend has it (and this tale has been validated for me by City fans) that Imre Varadi, a British player of Hungarian heritage, had been affectionately renamed Imre *Banana* by some of the City support. Prompting fans to turn up to matches with inflatable bananas. Although these inflatable bananas were being taken to matches in an era of monkey chants and banana skins thrown at black players during football matches, I have it on good authority that the birth of the inflatables craze was more a case of mildly xenophobic mispronunciation, as opposed to racially motivated antagonism. Either way, it is not especially funny. Not even in a surreal sense. City fans point to the 1988-89 season as the pinnacle of their inflatable dalliance, as they made their side-splitting way across the Pennines to play Hull City at the start of that season, armed with only their balloons and a tremendous propensity to fail.

Another example of that *famous* City sense of humour is the recently adopted goal celebration by fans: The Poznań. Although it's been a popular goal celebration in Eastern Europe since the early 1960s, City were first introduced to it in late 2010 during a UEFA Europa League game against Lech Poznań. Initially unimpressed with the opposing Polish fans using it against them when turning around, linking shoulders and bouncing up and down on the spot as a way of marking their team's goal, a month or so later City fans had adopted the celebration and continue to use it (Celtic and Rangers have similar goal celebrations), leaving the rest of us to revel in their comedic majesty.

Damien Costello spent most of the rest of that 1989-90 season in his greying T-shirt. At the end-of-year disco he turned up with his inflatable banana, and I have no doubt that Damien has indulged in a Poznań or two since, the hilarious little shit. It's much harder for me to try to imagine Damien Costello as a naturally charismatic winner. It's difficult for me to try and visualise how Damien would feel about the financial position of City *now*, since he spent much of our time at secondary school whining about financial injustice and civic receptions in Old Trafford.

Which brings us to 2008.

A decade earlier, City were playing third-tier football and boasting of superior fan loyalty and spectacular attendance figures. However, 2008 saw the purchase of Manchester City by the Abu Dhabi United Group. This takeover was accepted in uncustomary good spirits by City fans, who took to standing outside their stadium on the day of the takeover with more of that good-natured xenophobia in the guise of tea towels tied on heads by way of welcome to their new owner, Sheikh Mansour bin Zayed Al Nayhan.

It would be churlish of me to write about Manchester City without mentioning their recent Premiership League Title victory– their first league title win in 44 years. A spectacular Aguero finish delivered the title to City – a title we'd effectively handed over by throwing away an impressive points lead towards the end of the season. Despite my reluctance to accept them as our greatest rivals, we definitely did not enjoy their victory. It was painful. Painful because we could no longer count down the years of failure on the Old Trafford banner, painful because we were so close to victory, but mostly painful because every United fan knew we'd never hear the bastard *end of it*.

It's a funny thing though, because I honestly think the 1989 victory was feasted on more voraciously. I've seen Costello's T-shirt on other City fans decades after the event. There's something within them that means they'll always have their eye on us. No matter what they achieve it'll always be with a beady, watchful eye on Manchester United, and this is what keeps them small time.

Since City's league victory, the media like to paint Manchester as the most important city in football. They speak about the dawning of a new era in which both teams will now be the country's footballing powerhouses; how each season will essentially be a battle between the red and blue sections of this fair city. But there are two major stumbling blocks preventing a Mancunian rivalry for any significant length of time. The first is City's obsession with United, which has served, and will only serve, to undermine them. The second stumbling block is that City, in the last few years, have become everything they claimed to stand against. For years their fans stated that they hadn't won because they have been "authentic." Or that they have no silverware because they "can't afford to buy it". Only now of course, they *do* have the money and they *are* buying it. And if truth be told, I think City are *at least* as uncomfortable with winning on those terms as we are watching them win.

City are confused; having taken the moral high ground on the football finance issue and Mancunian authenticity (Etihad is not a Mancunian suburb, nestled between Ladybarn and Fallowfield, no matter what they tell you), they are divided on key issues like the management of Tevez, and even their newfound success. But despite this identity crisis, United will always see City for what they are.

When you go into work on a Monday morning, trying desperately to avoid the bore who's determined to tell you about their weekend in tremendous detail – without picking up on the clues you exhibit to show your displeasure? *That's City.*

When Derby Day comes, it's not so much *The Clash of the Titans*, as being forced to share a stuffy staff room with someone eating cheese and onion crisps, all the while waxing lyrical about Coldplay. Unpleasant? Absolutely. *That's City.*

Which is why they'll *never* be our greatest rivals, and always just the *Nosey* Neighbours.

Lucia Zanetti is the luckiest mam that ever lived. Not only that, she has had the good fortune to support the greatest football team in the world during their glory years. If it helps, she's yet to win the National Lottery. She blogs at nobodylikesasmartarse.wordpress.com.

SIXTEEN

KEEP THE RED FIRES BURNING
BY JOSHUA MAJOR

'WHAT DOESN'T KILL YOU makes you stronger', so the saying goes, and it's something I firmly believe. United are a club whose history is littered with examples of triumph over adversity; it's a theme that makes the club all the more appealing to fans around the world.

I wrote this essay shortly after I learned that I had made the last two from an original 80+ applicants for a job I wanted; but in the end they chose the other candidate. After playing the game with my potential employers over the course of four interviews, I was told I was good *enough*, but they went with someone *slightly better*. It felt very much like when Sergio Aguero destroyed our title dreams with a flash of his right boot; ostensibly the last meaningful kick of the season in the final minute of the final game. Heartbroken doesn't begin to describe how I felt then, nor how I felt about the job. To come so close and have it wrenched from within your grasp in such dramatic fashion is, to say the least, gutting.

As fans, we stick it out through troubled times: we look forward to the day when "we" can put things right. It's always "we"; even though when you're sitting in the stands you know you can't influence games, but you are in it together with the team. You shout, you scream, you will the players to run that extra yard, make that last-ditch tackle and put in that little bit extra effort to get the goal the team so badly needs. The deafening noise in the Stretford End makes it feel as though it could almost suck the ball into the net. More often than not, the players respond and we cheer as the Stretford End reverberates, and the "Reds go marching on, on, on".

More than any other club in world football, Manchester United is defined as much by its low points as by its successes. Perhaps, more importantly, United are defined by their ability to bounce back, to rise up against adversity and show that our true strength lies in our togetherness and indomitable spirit. From a bond forged within the club itself, with players and staff alike; from fans who consistently attend games and sing their hearts out, one thing is certain: United's strength comes from our unified stand.

In today's game (even with the Glazers in charge), we find ourselves a financial behemoth, raking in revenue from all over the world. We have enjoyed an unprecedented period of success over the last 20 years or so. We've watched the best players in world football come and play for us. None of these things are the source of our strength. That comes from our philosophy and our history of never giving up. It comes from always playing with pride and respecting what has gone before us. Our strength lies in our togetherness, that which we have shown both on and off the pitch.

These are the things that keep United going when the going gets tough; these are the things that keep the supporters singing. Success, trophies and marketing will always attract fans, but the ones who stay, even when we're not winning, *especially* when we're not winning, do so for the love of the club and – importantly – for the love of its history.

There are countless examples of fans being at odds during the turbulent times in our past: single games used as examples designed to show the club's rise in a questionable light. Throughout history we have often been accused of trying to 'do things the hard way'. Yet one of our greatest successes was born from our worst ever low. Winning the European Cup in 1968, 10 years after the Munich disaster, was an immeasurably brilliant achievement. I cannot imagine how people felt in 1958 when they heard the news of the plane crash that took the lives of 20 people: footballers, journalists, fans; all friends and family to someone, somewhere.

From the ashes of that disaster United rose, led with distinction by Sir Matt Busby. In 1968, his work paid off as a new team, Busby's Babes, won the European Cup. They were the first English team to do so and they did it with style, panache and flair. Players like Best, Charlton and Law grabbed the headlines that year (although Law did not play in the final), but the entire team was full of outstanding talent: Foulkes, Brennan, Stepney, Stiles, Kidd, Dunne, Sadler and Crerand all played that night, and all are names synonymous with United.

After the tragedy of 1958, the joy felt by fans watching as those players lifted the European Cup 10 years later must have been immense, perhaps even similar to our unprecedented– and still unique – treble win in 1999.

Following the European Cup triumph in 1968, the club went through a barren period, culminating in our relegation in 1974 to the second tier of English football for the first time since 1937. To rub salt in the wounds, it was Denis Law, a United hero, who sealed our fate. While the myth says it was his goal that relegated us, in fact, we needed to win the game, and we also needed Birmingham to lose theirs in order to have a chance of survival. Birmingham won, thus rendering our result meaningless. But, to have a former hero back-heel a goal and effectively confirm our relegation, while playing for our biggest rivals, must have been nigh on impossible to take.

It would have been easy for the club to wallow in self-pity and for the fans to lose faith. After all, it was a period of struggle for the team in footballing terms, and difficult to accept that United were now playing in the Second Division, a league they didn't belong in. Nonetheless, once again, United's strength came to the fore; attendances actually increased during the following season as the team went on to win the Second Division title by two points.

Attendances swelled from an average of 42,712 to 48,389 during the 1973-74 season as we battled our way through the Second Division. This was the highest attendance figure in the country and even higher than

Division One title winners, Liverpool, who managed an average gate of 45,966. United fans continued to watch their team and support them through the relegation, their swollen numbers proving my contention that it's the bad times, the times of adversity, that bring us closer together.

Speaking of adversity, Eric Cantona was, and still is, loved by United fans around the world and much has been written about the man. He hit the depths of despair on 25 January 1995 when he retaliated against a Crystal Palace fan's insults by famously launching a flying kick into his chest. Cantona was arrested and convicted of assault and served an eight-month ban imposed by the Football Association. That season, United lost out on the title, with Cantona's absence a considerable and decisive factor.

In his comeback game against Liverpool the great man simply picked up where he'd left off – setting up a goal for Nicky Butt in the second minute, before scoring a penalty himself. That season he led United to a League and Cup double, scoring the winner against Liverpool in the FA Cup final. United were the first team ever to win the double twice. How's that for triumph!

The last 20 years have seen a period of sustained dominance in the domestic league as well as a couple of memorable Champions League wins. This has no doubt attracted millions of new followers worldwide – and who could blame them? Led by players like Roy Keane, Bryan Robson and Eric Cantona, it is fair to say United's leaders were also born winners and typified the United attitude: we never give up until the final whistle blows.

Realistically, the blow of losing last season's title to our local rivals was massive and hit us hard. Despite only losing out on goal difference, and with almost the final kick of the season, it is viewed as one of our lowest points by many fans – especially the younger generation who are so used to winning. Many, however, will remember the 26-year wait before Sir Alex Ferguson won his first Premier League title in 1993. What the younger generation might not realise is that *without* these lows, the highs wouldn't feel nearly so good. As fans, we stick by our team throughout. Some say it's easier to do that when you're winning. Not for me. Losses, lows, disappointments; I believe these things unite us. José Mourinho used 'siege mentality' effectively at Chelsea and Inter Milan, so shall we endure as United fans. We will stand, a stronger collective after the disappointment of last season.

This applies to the players too. The disappointment and pain felt in the final seconds of last season can only fuel the desire and motivation to fight on and make sure it is not repeated. Our players will not want to feel like that again: it was a tough, but vital, learning experience for the youngsters in the squad.

"What doesn't kill you makes you stronger."

I'm sure this group of players will show the mental strength required to bounce back in the exemplary fashion that characterises this club: United, we never give up.

Joshua Major is a United fan of 30 years standing, finally becoming a season ticket holder in 2012. He writes his own blog, Busbysbeard.wordpress.com, and can be found on Twitter ranting about United, football and beards - @BusbyMUFC.

SEVENTEEN

AFTER THE GOLDRUSH
BY PAUL REEVE

PREDICTIONS OF DYNASTIES AND decades of domination are commonplace in football. A couple of trophies or a spell of lavish spending leads to pundits and experts alike lining up to greet the dawning of a new era and to pen premature obituaries. In the last 15 years we've seen United, Arsenal, Chelsea and, most recently (and sickeningly), City proclaimed the top team in English football, with each supposedly having the infrastructure and personnel in place to guarantee lasting superiority for years to come.

Football never quite works out like that though. Anyone who has ever attempted to make money gambling on the sport knows there are simply too many variables that make predicting the future an almost impossible task. As supporters, we consider ourselves knowledgeable (sage-like, in numerous cases) and we like to think we have a handle on what's likely to occur. But, ultimately, we're completely and utterly in the dark as to what'll happen from one year to the next. Therein lies the base, soap-opera-style appeal of the game – a familiar format with an ever-evolving cast of characters, storylines, outcomes and cliffhangers.

Predictably, therefore, it was a commonly held belief that United would go on to dominate football after winning the treble. Domestically at least, that looked to be a correct assumption, given the manner in which we strolled to the title, with four games to spare, in April 2000. Defending our European title proved a bridge too far, but there was no disgrace in losing to eventual winners, Real Madrid, at the quarter final stage. Overall, it was a season we cruised through. After the manic, rollercoaster ride of the previous campaign, which saw our collective lifetimes' ambitions fulfilled, it wasn't exactly difficult to endure watching your team smash everyone in sight and cruise to the title while scoring 97 goals.

With home success now a given, things clearly needed freshening up if we were ever to witness a repeat European triumph. In the summer of 2001 this was done in some style, with the acquisitions of Ruud van Nistelrooy and Juan Sebastián Verón, arguably the best in their positions in Europe at the time. Having announced his intention to retire at the end of the season, this double swoop appeared to signal Fergie's intention to go out in style. However, within days of completing the protracted Verón negotiations came the baffling announcement that Jaap Stam was being shipped off to Lazio – and, even more bafflingly, he was to be replaced by Laurent Blanc. Stam, we were later informed, had allegedly "lost a little bit" in Ferguson's eyes. Larry White's early performances confirmed that United's defence had lost an awful lot more.

United were still scoring freely while van Nistelrooy settled in quickly and looked the part from the off. The problem was at the other end, where only five clean sheets were recorded in the league before the turn of the year. Having shone throughout the previous season, Fabien Barthez was now making regular gaffes, his response to which was a doomed attempt to confound criticism by taking an even greater number of outlandish risks. Defeats to Liverpool, Arsenal, and Chelsea in the run-up to Christmas left us down in seventh and out of the picture in title terms, so attention was focused on a potential European final in Glasgow to provide Fergie's fitting finale.

After seeing off Deportivo in the quarters, only Bayer Leverkusen stood between United and a meeting with Real Madrid in a Hampden Park final. Despite us taking the lead in both legs, the Germans scraped through on away goals and thus denied Fergie his dream send-off. It was a tie we should have won, and one that still rankles to this day. Leverkusen were a decent side with good players, but clearly a team punching above their weight who were never going to enjoy repeat success at such a level. Defeat in the tie represented a huge, missed opportunity and proved too much of a low for Fergie to contemplate retiring on.

Having been demolished 6-1 at OT the previous February, Arsenal ended 2001-02 as double winners and the nation was able to let out a collective sigh of relief. Three successive league titles at the start of the decade had cemented United's position as the most hated team in the country. This was the era of the ABU and it was a situation that we, as fans, were entirely comfortable with. Despite the rapid growth of the club, and despite it becoming the commercial behemoth we see today, the bond between supporters and players has remained remarkably solid. Although David Beckham had become a bona fide global superstar, he was still seen as a boyhood Red, living the dream. There were frequent gripes about day-trippers, rising ticket prices and Diego Forlan's inability to control a football, but on the whole we'd enjoyed a spectacular few seasons.

So, it was a revitalised Fergie who signed on for another three years and set about wrestling back the title from Arsenal. Or, perhaps more pertinently, from Arsène Wenger, with whom he enjoyed a relationship that could more accurately be described as a very public, mutual loathing. The first order of business was the signing of Rio Ferdinand as a 12-month overdue replacement for Stam. That was quickly followed by the departure of Dwight Yorke, a man seemingly unconcerned with the daily demands of playing professional football for Manchester United, certainly since he'd first laid eyes on Katie Price's impressive cleavage.

With Ruud once again playing like a man on a mission, stellar supporting roles from Giggs and Scholes – together with notable shifts from Silvestre and O'Shea in his debut season – United won back the title following a thrilling tussle with Arsenal. The celebrations at Goodison Park on the final day were raucous, and Fergie's decision to stay on appeared vindicated. United were back in their rightful place. The disappointment of the previous campaign could be put down to the fact that the players had been distracted by his aborted retirement, the manager explained.

Some 12 months later, however, the triumphant conclusion of the previous season was just a distant memory. Although the season ended with a day out in Cardiff, an FA Cup win didn't quite cut it after 10 years of title races and competing for the big prize in Europe. Beckham and Verón were sold during the close season and the twin disasters of Eric Djemba-Djemba and Kleberson brought in – an ill-judged attempt to replace a pair of purring Rolls Royces with a couple of punctured unicycles.

Ferguson brought an action against the Coolmore Stud in November 2003. Despite most fans siding with him initially, the legal action resulted in increased murmurings of discontentment and accusations of greed – which were further fuelled by the May 2004 broadcast of a damning BBC documentary detailing alleged nepotistic dealings with son Jason's Elite Sports agency. Rio Ferdinand's explanation that he simply "forgot" to take a drugs test (that resulted in him serving an eight-month ban) didn't exactly endear him to supporters either.

In spite of finishing a lowly third and getting knocked out of Europe by a Porto side managed by some wannabe upstart named Mourinho, there were, however, some positives. Ruud continued to score for fun and we'd also brought in Bellion and Dong, which must have come as major comfort to Diego Forlan, as it meant he was no longer the biggest laughing stock at the club. Another bright spot was the arrival of Cristiano Ronaldo, the adolescent version, characterised by terrible highlights, rampant acne and an unerring ability to fall over at the slightest touch – far removed from the strutting, sculpted Adonis he became a couple of years later.

The following season provided little respite from the gathering storm clouds. Smith, Heinze and Rooney all came in, while treble stalwart Nicky Butt headed to Newcastle and, mercifully, the much-lampooned Forlan was offloaded to Villarreal. Newly installed at the Abramovich-bankrolled Chelsea, Mourinho's charges swept to the title with a record points total, having lost only one game all season. The 14 wins and three draws from November to March briefly appeared to have dragged United back into the picture, but any faint hopes of catching the cockneys were extinguished by defeats away to Norwich and Everton during April.

Alan Smith and Gabriel Heinze – full-blooded if

finesse-free players – were initially welcomed into the fold, as they at least added some steel to United's team. Compared with the combative, never-say-die spirit demonstrated by Chelsea, we appeared light-weight and ineffective. Darren Fletcher wasn't convincing anyone at this point. Quinton Fortune still featured regularly and the likes of Miller, Kleberson and Djemba-Djemba were clearly never going to make it at OT. Although we had Ronaldo and Rooney to enjoy, it speaks volumes about our declining fortunes that Heinze, with his penchant for ear-splitting wolf-whistles and habitual tendency to get caught out of position, was the recipient of the Fans' Player of the Year Award for 2005.

Most of the talk during the second half of the season was not concentrated on pitch matters, however, as the spectre of an aggressive takeover bid from the Glazer family loomed large. The directors and the manager, like the fans, appeared to be taking a unified stance against such a prospect until it became clear, as the season ebbed to a close, that our days as a PLC were numbered. After years of buying up shares and clinging to the pipedream of supporter representation at board level, instead we were to become the plaything of a rich American, intent on lining his pockets and bankrolling an ailing business empire with 'our' profits. Regular supporter gripes concerning team selections and tactics were replaced by an array of emotions ranging from glum acceptance to outright fury – United's future was being mortgaged right before our eyes.

If Fergie felt under pressure during the summer of 2005, he certainly didn't admit as much in public. His record over the years ensured that he continued to enjoy the bulk of matchgoers' support, but for a large and loud minority there was still a stinging sense of betrayal, one that persists to this day. The feeling was that Ferguson, having been happy to lend his support to fans' groups in direct opposition to the takeover, was rather too quick to perform an about-turn and seemingly give his blessing to the new owners on their arrival. As custodian of the club and all it stands for, perhaps if he'd remained true to his principles he could have threatened to walk and maybe even stopped the takeover altogether. Instead, he explained, his actions were dictated by a sense of loyalty to his staff, and had nothing to do with self-preservation and a reputed four million a year salary.

By the close of the year, ongoing discontentment had developed into full-blown despair at the direction in which the club appeared to be headed. After a bright start to the season, United soon found themselves trailing Chelsea again, following a poor performance in the home derby from which we were fortunate to escape with a single point. Then, after an uninspiring draw at Anfield, a turgid home defeat to Blackburn led to stinging criticism of the players and the tactics being employed.

The 4-5-1 system, using Van Nistelrooy as a lone(ly) striker, was seen as the brainchild of head coach Carlos Quieroz. Although its adoption was viewed with some suspicion, it was generally accepted that the tried and tested 4-4-2 had flopped in Europe and left us somewhat exposed in midfield, given that we no longer had a youthful, all-action Roy Keane at our disposal. Utilising 4-5-1 in the San Siro or Bernabeu was one thing, but lining up against bog-standard, Premier League flotsam with this system felt like an affront to our history and traditions of attacking football.

The wheels well and truly came off during a seismic few days following an abysmal 4-1 defeat at Middlesborough. Despite having missed the match through injury, it was Roy Keane's turn to provide commentary for video highlights of United's latest performance on MUTV – and to say he didn't hold back is something of an understatement. Although never aired, Keane tore into his colleagues, with Smith, Richardson and Fletcher bearing the brunt of his considerable ire; he delivered a crushing assessment of their performances and vented angrily at the general malaise surrounding the team.

Keane, in a move tantamount to gross insubordination, had pushed his long-fractious relationship with Ferguson to the limit and would depart the club a fortnight later. Heading to Paris alongside seven thousand other Reds, as the details of the story were still emerging, there was no doubt who United's supporters were backing. Finally, there was evidence that our feelings of disillusionment were shared by a prominent figure within the club. Admittedly, it probably wasn't best advised for the club captain to round on his teammates so spectacularly, but at least there was now an acknowledgement of what had become increasingly clear in our minds over several months.

A gloomy night in Paris, that saw United crash to CL minnows Lille, was followed by what was probably the performance of the season, a hard-earned 1-0 win over Chelsea that saw the team regain some pride after what had been a miserable week. Indeed, it could be said that Keanegate had a very positive effect, given that United only lost a further three league games from November onwards. It was, nevertheless, a season peppered with humiliations: finishing bottom of the group in the CL; drawing at Burton (after which there was a feeling among some overzealous, conspiracy theorists that a home replay was desired so that United could collect the gate receipts); a chaotic defeat at Eastlands, where Evra was substituted at HT on his debut, hot on the heels of which came defeat at Anfield in the FA Cup.

Ferguson pointed to the fact that United ended 2005-06 with a trophy, but surely only the most deluded United fans took any solace from beating Wigan in the final of the Carling Cup. Rumours of a bust-up with the much-loved Van Nistelrooy proved accurate when he was sold to Madrid for what seemed like an absurdly low £10 million fee. The previous January we'd added Nemanja Vidic and Patrice Evra (both of whom looked terrible, based on what we'd seen of their performance up to that point). They were followed by the only summer signing, Michael Carrick, picked up for a 'bargain' £18 million when he'd been available for around £3.5 million only two years previously. All in all, it was difficult to comprehend Ferguson's thinking at this point.

On the eve of the 2006-07 season, a piece appeared in *The Guardian*, written by Rob Smyth, summing up the overriding sense of doom that gripped many of United's supporters. The article was an unflinching analysis of MUFC post-takeover and pointedly accused Ferguson of "shredding his legacy at every turn". It described a club no longer able to attract top players; a squad that was a "baggy mess of has-beens, never-will-bes and Liam Miller", and an aged manager, struggling to come to terms with the "sarong-wearing, pink champagne swigging" lifestyle of the modern day footballer. And yes, it made for marvellous reading for us naysayers – none of us prepared, quite honestly, for the remarkable turnaround in fortunes we were to witness over the following 10 months.

There was no key decision or pivotal move that led to Ferguson meeting the challenge of Chelsea head on, as United regained the title in 2007, merely an unswerving belief in his own decisions and faith in the players he had assembled. Free of the brooding presence of Van Nistelrooy, Rooney and Ronaldo blossomed as United became fun to watch once more. Darren Fletcher grew into the player only the most ardent Fergie loyalist could ever have predicted and, defensively, Vidic and Evra proved that a combined fee of £12 million for the pair was a masterstroke rather than a joke. Some 12 months later as we were crowned European Champions, following yet another league title, Sir Alex's doubters were silenced for good.

Paul Reeve has watched United for over 30 years, holding a season ticket since it became a necessity after the Stretford End was demolished. Having previously contributed to *Red Issue*, he now writes a monthly column in *Red News* and can be also be found on - www.carlosartorial.wordpress.com

EIGHTEEN

A GLOBAL EMPIRE
BY WILL TIDEY

"Before the tragedy at Munich, the club belonged to Manchester. But afterwards, Manchester United captured the imagination of the entire world."

WHAT DOES IT MEAN to be a Manchester United supporter in 2012? It's a question we could put to the global fan base, estimated to be at 660 million, but the majority of answers would require translation. Remarkably, a football club that started life as an amateur outlet for railway workers in the late 19th century, has enlisted a red army of millions and has become the most powerful brand in sport today.

United have more than 200 official supporters' clubs, dotted throughout the world. They include branches in Gauteng, Indonesia, Bahrain, America, Canada, Bulgaria and Cyprus. There's one in Gorton, Manchester, in case you were wondering, and those who go regularly will tell you that Old Trafford retains a sense of community fostered by those who live and breathe the city United make their home in. But, there can be no hiding the fact that hometown fans are now in a very small minority – albeit an enduringly vocal one.

There remains a Mancunian heartbeat to Manchester United, but the blood coursing through the club's veins comes in all types, and from all places. Visit Old Trafford on match day and Manchester still looms large – with banners draped over the Stretford End, a reminder of the club's heritage and the people of the north-west who gave it to the world. "Manchester is my heaven" reads one. "For every Manc a religion" reads another. Supporters come and drink together in the beer-soaked, Manc-infused pubs surrounding the stadium; they stand and sing proudly of their city together, like they always have and always will. But, over time, they've come to accept that among them there could just as well be a United fan from Singapore as one from Salford.

Old Trafford is "the theatre of dreams" now. It's a football stadium posing as a global entertainment venue and many will have travelled thousands of miles to get there. Tourists take pictures; United's megastore is a frantic hive of excitable souvenir hunters, and corporate clients (Roy Keane's "prawn sandwich brigade") fill the best seats in the house.

Rivals used to joke that all United's fans lived in London. These days they're more likely to come from Tokyo or Shanghai, with almost half of United's gargantuan support said to be watching on from the Asia-Pacific region. Walk down any street, anywhere in the world, and the chances are you'll see a United shirt. You'll also find a bar showing United games and, whatever the hour, be greeted by a selection of nomadic Reds ready to watch them with you. Some will tell you Old Trafford is wherever you want it to be.

Take Nevada Smith's in downtown New York City: the perfect example. I was there for a Manchester derby once and walked through the doors at 7am to be greeted by at least 200 rowdy Reds singing United songs and knocking back lager for breakfast. Manchester was 3,000 miles away, but its heart and soul was on the east coast of America that morning, as expats rubbed shoulders with any number of nationalities and shared in the sweet taste of victory – red over blue.

The same scene unfolds in bars all over the world. United are everywhere; they are inescapable. They are readily accessible in all but the world's most remote places and it's almost impossible to live a life that doesn't, in some way, include them. That's the level of fame and influence we're talking about here – a brand so strong it can infiltrate the daily lives of people who don't even *like* football.

If you flew out of Heathrow in August 2012, you will have seen United's stars on a billboard the size of a penalty area. If you used the DHL website you'll have come upon the club's logo and some of United's best-known faces on their home page. If you logged onto Facebook there's a good chance you or one of your friends will have been among the 27 million fans of the official Manchester United page. If you walked past a newsagent you'll have seen news of Robin van Persie's signing on the front page. If you turned on the news, you will have been told about it.

United's reach is remarkable, and ever-expanding. With every globetrotting, pre-season tour, thousands of new disciples are born. United continue to expand with the airing of each match they are involved in;

with every marketing campaign that trades on their name, and every time they make the news. Put simply, United are the football club it's most likely you cannot help fall in love in with. Glory hunters? Prospective United fans are the hunted now.

To explore why, we must first revisit the tragedy that unfolded on 6 February 1958, on a snow-covered runway at Munich Airport – with United on their way back from a European Cup quarter-final against Red Star Belgrade, a team very much in the ascendancy. Eight Manchester United players lost their lives as a result of the crash on take-off, along with three members of staff and eight journalists. Through unspeakable tragedy, United found their way into the hearts of the world.

"Before the tragedy at Munich, the club belonged to Manchester," reads a plaque by the players' entrance at Old Trafford. "But afterwards, Manchester United captured the imagination of the entire world."

My dad is one of many United fans whose allegiance was born out of the Munich disaster. As a boy of six, he found himself overwhelmed by the public outpouring of sympathy and the coming together of the football community to support United in their time of need. "It felt like everyone in football was behind United after the disaster," he says. "Their story led the news for weeks and by the end of the season everyone in the country was willing them on." Matt Busby's men were seeking a third successive league title that season. They were through to the semi-finals of the European Cup and the fifth round of the FA Cup. History beckoned, but the cruellest of fates intervened, and a football club's grief would be played out before an audience of millions. It was an achievement to have finished the season at all, but to reach the FA Cup final – where they lost 2-0 to Nat Lofthouse's Bolton – was testament to a fighting spirit that would become United's enduring legacy.

Busby's team were a universal symbol of hope. Drawing strength from adversity, they emerged from the spectre of that fateful night in Munich to become the most glorious champions of Europe a decade later. When it comes to romantic sporting tales to hang a brand on, it simply doesn't get any better. And the fact that United conquered while playing expressive, attacking football – inspired by the likes of Charlton, George Best and Denis Law – served to enhance their appeal to the masses.

Best's role in spreading the gospel of United cannot be underestimated. The incomparable Northern Irishman was equal parts rock star and footballer, and with his demolition of Eusebio's Benfica in March

1966 arrived a new sporting sensation. Best was just 19 when he led United to a famous 5-1 victory that night. "El Beatle" had taken the stage and Manchester United had what we might call today 'a face for their brand'. Best wasn't just a football icon, he was a cultural phenomenon who took the red shirt to places it had never been before.

Those heady days in the 1960s attracted United admirers from all over the world and paved the way for the aggressive marketing we see today: a prelude to the commercial revolution that would take hold three decades later.

The 1990s brought a new frontier for football in England. With the birth of the Premier League, and Sky's injection of TV money, came new revenue streams and new opportunities for clubs to expand their global horizons. Some clubs failed to take advantage, but United were ravenous and prepared. They floated on the stock exchange in 1991, to a value of £18 million, and made it a priority to aggressively attract new fans from every corner of the planet.

"It's easy to forget that, at that time, United were the only global brand in the Premiership," says Nigel Currie, director of sports marketing and sponsorship firm brandRapport, who has worked on deals between Vodafone and United. "There was a fight going on between the big representatives of the major European leagues to see who'd come out on top, and United were intent on winning it.

"The timing of United's recent success was important. Had the internet been around, or had the rush to develop huge global brands been prevalent in the 1980s, Liverpool would undoubtedly have got so far ahead of the other clubs in terms of popularity and commercial appeal that they would have been hard to catch," Currie adds.

Soon enough United's ambition as a business entity was matched by that of Sir Alex Ferguson's team on the pitch. In 1993, Ferguson masterminded the club's first league title success in 26 years, and launched a dynasty perfectly timed to coincide with the dawn of the Premier League era. English football had opened its doors to the world, and the world watched on as Ferguson's red and white army marched forward and recaptured the spirit of the great Busby team.

United games were by now being televised globally. A new generation of iconic players rose to fame, and players like Ryan Giggs, Eric Cantona and, most notably, David Beckham, became household names (with Beckham becoming arguably the most marketable United player – and perhaps the most marketable athlete – of them all).

United had been a limited company for a century, but now they were big business. In 1998 Rupert Murdoch's BSkyB tried to capitalise it with a £623 million takeover bid that valued the club at more than 30 times the amount Michael Knighton had sought to buy them for in 1989. United accepted the offer, but Murdoch's bid was eventually nixed by the Monopolies and Mergers Commission, who feared Sky's role in negotiating TV rights would lead to United having an unfair advantage. United fans, on the whole, were mightily relieved. But it proved to be merely a stay of execution.

In the meantime, there was a return to European glories. United's historic treble season culminated with the most dramatic of triumphs in the 1999 Champions League final and, as a by-product, sent the club's global brand value soaring higher still.

United's men in suits weren't about to let this opportunity pass them by. The following season a four-year, £30 million sponsorship deal was inked with Vodafone, which not only put the telecoms giant on United's shirts but also allowed them to use the United name to sell their own products and services. "There is additional business potential in bringing together the world's largest telecommunications company and the world's best-known football club," said Vodafone chief executive Peter Bamford. It was a deal ahead of its time.

There was more to come. In November 2000, United signed a record-breaking £302.9 million kit manufacturing, merchandising and sponsorship deal with Nike. It came to fruition in 2002 and has been worth around £25 million per season to United ever since. When it runs out in 2015, United can expect to break records again. But above and beyond the big sums of cash, the club gained huge global exposure from their association with Nike – as indeed they have from no end of other corporate tie-ins and sponsorship arrangements that they've brokered since they sealed the 2002 deal.

Who'd have thought 20 years ago they'd be selling Thai beer at Old Trafford? Singha is the only lager you can buy at some of the bars inside the stadium, while the club's official wine supplier ships bottles in from Chile, and United's "responsible drinking" partner is – rather ironically you'd think – Russian vodka maker, Smirnoff. United's "official snack partner" is Malaysian outfit Mister Potato; Swiss manufacturer Hublot is the club's "official timekeeper", while Turkish Airlines is the club's "official airline partner". If that's not global branding, then I don't know what is.

But it's the heavyweight influence of the American sponsors that looms largest – with Nike making the famous shirts now emblazoned with the name of insurance company AON. There was a time when we thought America didn't get "soccer". These days they provide United's largest sponsors, a regular pre-season destination and an ever-growing audience, ripe for indoctrination. They also provide the club's owners, of course.

The (bloody) Glazers. Where Rupert Murdoch failed, a billionaire family from Florida succeeded; this time the idea was to buy United largely on credit and let the club finance a mountain of debt with its profits.

For many, the unrest runs deeper than the potentially catastrophic financial implications of Glazer rule. They see ownership by an American family with no particular affiliation to United as a symptom of a football club that has grown ever more willing to sell its soul. Some will tell you they gave up on United years ago for that very reason. Others are desperately clinging on to the faded identity of the football club they fell in love with in the first place – and are fighting to get it back.

But while some fans will spit bile in the direction of the Glazers until the day they walk out of Old Trafford, United's rampant thirst for global domination is not a condition they can be blamed for. The wheels were put in motion long before they arrived, when United's board decided on a course of action to attract the biggest fan base in football, and began plotting it with extravagant success. Perhaps they were wrong to do so. If they hadn't, United might still feel like it belonged to Manchester, and the Glazers might not have been tempted to invest in the first place. On the other hand, Old Trafford would not have witnessed the level of success it has had under the Ferguson regime – with much owed to the profits gained from United's increasingly global enterprise.

There is a compromise to be made by the modern football fan. If you want to watch players like Rooney, van Persie, and Shinji Kagawa, and if you want to watch winning football, then you must accept that there's a price to pay. The price is being part of a supporters' network that spans the globe, and in so doing, helps United to buy the success that you so crave. It might feel soulless at times, and it might not be how you once imagined it, but it's the only way football at the highest level can be maintained.

You could say United have sold out. You could say the success of their global brand is just the inevitable conclusion of what Busby started in the 1950s. Either way, as a United fan in 2012, you're one of hundreds of millions who cares.

Will Tidey is world football editor and lead writer at American website Bleacher Report, and the author of *Life with Sir Alex: A Fan's Story of Ferguson's 25 Years at Manchester United*. He was there in 1999.

NINETEEN

THE FLOWERS OF MANCHESTER
BY TOM CLARE

THE BRITISH EUROPEAN AIRWAYS Elizabethan aircraft was parked on the apron by the passenger terminal at Munich's Riem Airport. The time was 14:56 on Thursday, 6 February 1958. Inside the fuselage, the two stewardesses, Margaret Bellis and Rosemary Cheverton, and steward, Tommy Cable, were busy ensuring that the aircraft doors were secure, and that the 38 passengers were securely fastened into their seats. The atmosphere was subdued, tense, and some passengers were even frightened. During the previous 25 minutes there had been two attempts at take-off, both aborted because the pilots experienced surging in the aircraft engines. Some passengers changed seats, preferring to move to the back of the aircraft where they hoped, in the event of anything unusual happening, they would be safer.

On the flight deck, the two experienced pilots, Captains Ken Rayment and Jim Thain, were going through their pre-flight checks once more. Satisfied that all was well, the following communication took place between the pilots and the Munich Control Tower.

Elizabethan 609: Munchen Control Tower B-Line 609 Zulu Uniform – I am ready to taxi – Over.

Munchen Tower: 609 Zulu Uniform – Munchen Tower. Wind two nine zero – eight knots – cleared to runway two five – QNH one zero, zero four – Time five six and three quarters – Over.

Elizabethan 609: Thank you.

Elizabethan 609: Munich 609 Zulu Uniform – are we cleared to line up?

Munchen Tower: B-Line 609 Zulu Uniform – Cleared to line up and hold – And here is your clearance. Over.

Elizabethan 609: Roger – Go ahead.

Munchen Tower: Munchen Control clears B-Line 609 to the Manchester Airport via route as filed – maintain one seven thousand feet – right turn after take-off – climb on south course inbound Freising Range and maintain four thousand feet until further advised – Over.

Elizabethan 609: Roger – I understand. I am cleared to Manchester via the advised route to maintain seventeen thousand feet – a right turn out – the south course inbound to the Freising Range and maintain four thousand feet until further advised – Over.

Munchen Tower: Roger – Clearance correct.

Munchen Tower: B-Line 609 – What is your rate of climb? – Over.

Elizabethan 609: Six hundred feet a minute.

Munchen Tower: Ah ….. Roger.

Munchen Tower: B-Line 609 – Your clearance void if not airborne by 1504. Time now 1502.

Elizabethan 609: Roger – Understand valid until zero four.

Elizabethan 609: Ah, Munich – 609 Zulu Uniform is ready for take-off.

Munchen Tower: 609 – The wind three zero zero one zero knots – Cleared for take-off.

Elizabethan 609: Roger – Thank you

Munchen Tower: Munich Tower – Roger.

G-ALZU moved slowly out to the main runway and lined up. The aircraft's engines roared into life, the sound grew louder and louder until they reached their familiar high-pitched whine. Slowly, the big aircraft frame began to roll forward. It gathered speed, racing along like a high-powered motorcar – 70 knots, 80 knots, 90 knots – apprehension filled the passenger cabin as the aircraft thundered down the runway for the third time. Those passengers with window seats could see the thick slush being thrown up by the undercarriage as the aircraft powered along. Some passengers gripped the armrests on their seats tightly in fear. One cried out "We're all going to get fucking killed", another, "If this is death then I am ready for it."

In the cockpit, Thain was busy watching the instruments and calling out the ground speed as Rayment, the more experienced pilot, took charge of the aircraft controls. "105 knots, 110 knots." At 117 knots Thain called out "V1!" This was the decision speed, the point after which there is insufficient runway left to stop. G-ALZU was committed to take-off.

Thain's eyes concentrated on the groundspeed indicator and the next call should have been V2 at 119 knots, the minimum air speed required for lift-off. Instead, there was a rapid deceleration and the groundspeed dropped to 105 knots.

The end of the runway was before them. Rayment shouted, "Christ, we won't make it!" In seconds, the aircraft was 200 metres past the runway's end, tearing through the airport perimeter fencing and across the road beyond. Immediately in their path lay a house and a tree. The aircraft lurched to the right, colliding with the house. The impact tore the left wing off and ripped away part of the tail. The house burst into flames.

Out of control, the plane struck the tree and the port side of the cockpit ripped open. It travelled another 100 metres before the right fuselage hit a wooden garage containing a truck (this impact severed the complete tail section). The remains ploughed on for a further 70 metres before finally coming to a halt.

Inside the aircraft, the impacts had had a catastrophic effect on the passengers. A complete eerie silence descended. Of the 44 persons on board, 21 had already lost their lives. The time was just after 15:04.

The events of those long eight minutes in an aircraft on a foreign field in Bavaria were a defining moment in the history of Manchester United Football Club and brought to an end the short reign of arguably the finest football team the club has ever produced. This was the team affectionately known as the 'Busby Babes'. Little do people realise that those tragic eight minutes are more than partly responsible for the special link that exists today between Manchester United and their tribal following, which encircles the world.

Busby was farsighted. From the early days of his man-
agership he had recognised the value and importance
of taking the team overseas, allowing them to be seen;
he also recognised the value to the club of exploiting
foreign markets. After the Babes won that first league
championship, he fought the Football League authorities to allow Manchester United to enter the new European Cup competition, which had begun in 1955. He
could see the benefits of pitting his team's skills against
the best football clubs in Europe. By playing in the
competition, Busby could also see the financial benefits
that would accrue to the club; but more than that, he
wanted the prestige it would bring to the club throughout Europe. Where others feared to tread, Busby forged
ahead, and with his calm, but firm political nous and
manipulation he won the day. Had he not, who is to say
how long it would have been before English clubs were
allowed to take part in European competitions?

Matt Busby could be as hard as bell metal in his dealings with other clubs, or with the legislators of the game.
He fought his battles in a quiet, dogged, but determined
way. He was no pushover, as the authorities found out –
particularly the authoritarian Football League Secretary,
Alan Hardaker, who did all that he could to block Manchester United's entry into European football. Busby's
standing in the British game made him the patriarch

of his time. Sports writer, Hugh McIlvanney, wrote a piece at the time of Sir Matt's passing in 1994, later reproduced in his book *McIlvanney on Football*:

Greatness does not gad about, reaching for people in handfuls. It settles deliberately on a blessed few, and Matt Busby was one of them. If Busby had stood dressed for the pit, and somebody alongside him in the room had worn ermine, there would have been no difficulty about deciding who was special. Granting him knighthood did not elevate him. It raised however briefly, the whole dubious phenomenon of the honours system.

Busby emanated presence, substance, the quality of strength without arrogance. No man in my experience ever exemplified better the ability to treat you as an equal while leaving you with the sure knowledge that you were less than he was. Such men do not have to be appointed leaders. Some democracy of the instincts of the blood elects them to be in charge.

That innate distinction was the source of his effect on footballers. He never had to bully. One glance from under those eloquent eyebrows was worth ten bellows from more limited natures. Players did not fear his wrath. They dreaded his disapproval. His

judgement of the priorities of football was so sound,
his authority so effortless, that a shake of his head
inflicted an embarrassment from which the only
rescue was recovery of his respect.

On 12 September 1956, at the Park Astrid Stadium in Brussels, Manchester United became the first English league club to play in a European Cup football competition; on that occasion, they defeated Anderlecht RSC 2-0. However, it was the return leg just two weeks later that stimulated the imagination of the English football fan when the Babes defeated the Belgian club once again – but this time by the astonishing scoreline of 10-0. There followed games against German champions, Borussia Dortmund, and two epic confrontations with Spanish club, Athletic Bilbao, before they fell to, arguably, the greatest club side of its era, Real Madrid. European football greatly whetted the appetite of the English footballing public, and they wanted more of it.

During that same season, Manchester United were also firm favourites to become the first team in the 20th century to win what was then termed, 'the double' – achieved by winning both the league and the FA Cup. On Easter Saturday, 1957, the first part was completed when, after beating Sunderland at

Old Trafford, United retained the league title they had won so convincingly the year before. They also won through to the FA Cup Final, where they played Aston Villa. However, the 'double' was not to be. Just six minutes after the game at Wembley started, Peter McParland, the Aston Villa forward, made a horrific challenge on Ray Wood, the United goalkeeper, which effectively put him out of the game. In an era when no substitutes were allowed, Jackie Blanchflower took over in goal, and United played out the remaining 84 minutes with just 10 men. It was no surprise that when the final whistle blew, they had been beaten 2-1.

The following season saw this wonderful young team once again chasing the three trophies and the word 'treble' became an oft-heard expression among United fans. In the European Cup, Irish club, Shamrock Rovers and the Czech army club, Dukla from Prague, were both eliminated by the Babes. In early February 1958, the team was well placed to go on and win a third consecutive league championship and had progressed to the fifth round of the FA Cup. They had also reached the quarter-final of the European Cup where, in the first leg at Old Trafford, they defeated the Yugoslavian club Red Star Belgrade 2-1. There was buoyancy around the club, a feeling among both the players and the fans that the 'treble' was definitely on.

On 1 February 1958, United were involved in a game at Highbury against Arsenal. It turned out to be a classic, which they won 5-4, but little did anyone know that this would be the last time the Babes would play on English soil. The following Monday they flew out to Belgrade for their return game against Red Star. On Wednesday, 5 February 1958, in a game played out on a treacherous ice-bound pitch, United raced into a 3-0 half-time lead. The second half was a backs-to-the-wall effort as the Slavs pulled it back to 3-3, though United managed to hang on until the final whistle blew. They were through to the European Cup semi-final for the second successive year.

Sadly, this was to be the last game of football the Babes ever played together. This wonderful young team had been adventurous to the last. Less than 24 hours later they were torn apart inside the wreckage of an aircraft at the end of a German runway. They left the English game with a memorable example of their heady blend of skill, defiant determination, and entertaining football taught by Matt Busby.

Almost 55 years on the Busby Babes are still revered and remembered by Manchester United's legions of fans around the world. In footballing circles they are still talked about today. Over the years, their mystique and aura has strengthened. What made them so special, apart from the way that they played the game?

Well, they were a wonderful group of players, much loved and admired; yet they had their feet firmly set on the ground. There were no big egos, no prima donnas. They were very much the happy, uncynical, boy-next-door types, who lived life to the full. Their roots were tied into the northern industrial working class. The majority of the single boys lived in 'digs' and boarded in 'two-up, two-down' council houses, even though some of them were established international players. They were never seen in the media for the wrong reasons. They knew they were special, that's for sure, but it never affected them negatively. These were young men who would happily walk to the stadium before a game and willingly chat to the fans who paid to watch them play.

They were accessible to the people and to the Manchester United fans in particular; they were often seen out and about during the week, either at the local parks watching the schoolchildren playing football, or at the local shops, cinemas or dance halls. They attended prize-giving ceremonies for youth clubs. They certainly embraced the community and, without doubt, the community embraced them.

What might they have achieved had fate not dealt them such a cruel hand? Michael Parkinson, author and television celebrity, asked Sir Matt Busby the same question. It drew an immediate response;

"If they had entered it, they would have even won the Boat Race."

There is no more fitting testimony than that. It is difficult to convince today's generation just how good the Busby Babes team was, both collectively and individually. Does it matter? Not really, because those who did see them, saw their genius. They knew the Babes were the greatest team that Britain has ever produced and that their memory is imperishable. Those who followed them shared in their dream, and when they perished on that snow-filled runway at Munich, it left a huge chasm in their lives, one that was never filled. The Busby Babes were the pollinators of English football – they were 'The Flowers of Manchester.'

⎯⎯⎯⎯⎯⎯⎯⎯⎯⎯⎯⎯⎯⎯⎯⎯⎯⎯⎯⇍

Tom Clare was born in Manchester and grew up alongside the emergence of United's famous young team that became so widely known as the Busby Babes. He is the author of *Forever a Babe, Growing Up with Manchester United.*

TWENTY

LIFE:

WHAT HAPPENS TO YOU WHILE UNITED ARE BUSY MAKING OTHER PLANS

BY DANIEL HARRIS

THERE'S SOMETHING VERY WEIRD about peeling yourself off a pile-on and realising that, at 20 years old, from that second onwards things are only going to get worse. And if it's a pile-on in a Nou Camp gangway at 22.33 on 26 May 1999, then the realisation becomes an incontrovertible fact; for here resides the intersection of ecstasy and despair. Nothing will trump that moment; nothing you or United can do could trump that moment.

In 1998-99, the golden goose of club football was at its most delectably plump, the final season before its depressing descent into force-fed, depressive obesity. Each game was an event, and not just because United were playing; each one meant something, because the organisers understood that football was still the point. They were rewarded with a competition of shuddering intensity.

Priorities were different too: the aim? Get stuck into the finest teams around and see what happened, not just to win at all costs. The obsession was growing: in the mid-90s, league titles were as much about earning another go at Europe as anything else – but United were so far behind in the trophy-collecting stakes that winning none couldn't distract from the duty to provide joy and thrill. So, a group including Barcelona and Bayern Munich, with only one team guaranteed to qualify, was accepted with alacrity, and attacked accordingly.

And it gets worse. To spend any time with the treble winners is to experience unavoidable ire at the indolent, fraudulent cretins who comprise our team nowadays. But, given the misery that pollutes and defames our footballing lives these days, we're obligated to focus on the joy, so let's have a go. Here are three of the key games from United's greatest ever season:

ARSENAL AT VILLA PARK, FA CUP SEMI-FINAL REPLAY: 14 APRIL 2012

"Don't watch it alone", warned Ferguson, in the days when he cared what we did. "The more difficult it is, the more resilient they become", boasted Wenger, in the days when he said things because they were true, not because he was desperate to make them so.

There is an argument to be made that the 1999 FA Cup semi-final replay represents the zenith of football in this miserable country.

Rivalry and enmity had been building since the arrival of Arsène Wenger soon after the start of the 1996-97 season but, at that point, although top of the league, Arsenal were not considered a credible threat. Nor were they the following season, until they suddenly snatched the title with a murderously poetic post-January charge that surprised everyone, setting up the following season's duel between the two teams.

By the time they met at Villa Park, United led the league by a point and had a game in hand, but faced a marginally tougher run-in, with the added complication of a European Cup semi-final second leg. In any event, the encounter was boring, miserable and tight, and almost nothing happened, though even Martin Tyler had to acknowledge United's "long periods of superiority". Nonetheless, David Elleray still contrived the opportunity to make a bell of himself, accidentally disallowing a legitimate goal by his favourite player, revealing his profound feeling for the intricacies of the game.

By the time of the replay, the open net of a final with Newcastle tantalised as the reward for winning, but outside the ground, Paul Davis informed me that the score would be 3-0 to Arsenal. I decided to persevere. Incredibly, the match wasn't close to a sell-out, increasing the smuggery of the skint student with a £10 restricted view ticket – smuggery that was quickly punctured when they saw the United team. As was the case in the first game, Scholes was on the bench, but so too were Giggs and Yorke, with Cole left out altogether: this could never work.

Except, of course, that it could. Roy Keane stomped and pistoned around the pitch like Roy Keane in his pomp; like Roy Keane in his pomp against Arsenal, arms pumping, head doing its sideways motion, and United, deservedly, went in front on 17 minutes. Picking up the second ball after a long Schmeichel clearance was headed away, Beckham found Sheringham, who cleverly teed him up with a manoeuvre straight out of his captain's textbook, working the outside of his foot around the ball to earn some space away from Adams and the woolly-gloved Petit. But no one expected the astonishingly magnificent finish that came next, Beckham unleashing an out-swinging full-toss that shrieked past Seaman, done with the eyes from 25 yards. "What a goal!" gushed Tyler, but only after pausing to contemplate the implausibility of what he'd just seen.

Before the game, Beckham was one of the two players selected by Ferguson for a special word, the gist of which he explained to Hugh McIlvanney in *The Sunday Times* the following weekend:

"David, in his eagerness to have a crucial impact on a game, can occasionally over-elaborate. He has abilities that set him apart from every other player in Britain. Nobody else strikes the ball as well. The range and accuracy of his delivery, whether he is shooting, passing or putting over crosses, provide us with a weapon that is liable to win any match. In essence, my message to him was that he is at his deadliest when concentrating on the simple application of these tremendous skills." Best add 'good listener' to his long list of metrosexual credentials.

This was the first time Arsenal had been behind in a game since early January – in 17 games, they'd conceded only five goals – and like United, they were unbeaten in all competitions during the period. The beauty of the rivalry at this stage was that each party was convinced of its superiority, and so committed fully to attack, producing a minor classic at Old Trafford in February, and making the disappointment of the first game all the more acute.

On this occasion, United were dominant, wasting chances, with Solksjaer the principal culprit, uncharacteristically rushing a shot and *missing the target* when fed by Keane. Shortly afterwards, Blomqvist's effort was saved, following yet another pythagorean pass from Sheringham, before Solskjær showed his strength, holding off Keown, and hammering a trademark low shot close to the keeper's legs that looked an easy save but wasn't. Seaman hung on, but only just.

For Arsenal, Anelka snatched at a cross to lash high and wide, but when the equaliser appeared, it was out of nowhere; Bergkamp's shot from a distance deflected off Stam and scuttled past Schmeichel. While United replied almost immediately, Sheringham failed to connect with a low Beckham cross and for the first time Arsenal were in the game. Shortly afterwards, they thought they'd taken the lead when Schmeichel spilled another Bergkamp shot into the path of Anelka, who shuffled around him to tap it in. Unaware that the flag was up, Anelka was well into the crowd parading his magnificence with his friends when the terrible truth came to light, the United sections already swaying with laughter and thumbless hitchhikers. Given his first game antics, Elleray had no choice but to accede, but the subsequent delay made a mockery of Sheringham's Juve whinge of a week earlier; at 72.02 the ball crossed the line, celebrations continued until 72.33, and only at 72.48 was the verdict official.

Immediately afterwards, United were reduced to 10 men; an already-booked Keane slid in on Overmars. Determined to deny the referee the pleasure of flourishing a second yellow card and then a red, he turned on his heel. Equally determined to enjoy the pleasure of flourishing a second yellow card and then a red, Elleray set off in pursuit, but Keane was already halfway towards the tunnel, where, I later discovered, an old friend was one of hundreds of Arsenal supporters climbing over each other to flob at him.

United spent the remaining 17 minutes penned inside their own half as Arsenal went in search of a winner. They created little of note until, with seconds remaining, Parlour dragged himself outside Phil Neville who couldn't help but fold into a foul, conceding a penalty. Though Peter Schmeichel is the finest goalkeeper ever to toss an unnecessary bag into the back of a net (consider his almost Maradonaesque contribution to Denmark's European Championship win in 1992), his record at saving penalties was dismal (the UEFA Cup shootout against Torpedo Moscow in 1991-92; Everton away, League Cup 1993-94 and Sheringham at Spurs in 1994-95 was the extent of it). But cometh the hour cometh the future traitor: Bergkamp's firm but reachable effort was pushed aside and celebrated with a moment's elation before teammates were shooed away with great vengeance and furious anger. Extra-time.

If describing this game is trite, bothering to address what happened next is even more so, but here we are so here we are.

Arsenal burrowed forwards, intent on a winner, United attempted to hang on for penalties – Yorke loitered alone upfield and everyone else massed around the box. United's cause was not helped by the efforts of one RJ Giggs, Esq. who, on as a second-half substitute for Blomqvist, contrived a passing performance, careless even by his exalted standards. He was the second player identified as requiring a pre-match prod, as Ferguson subsequently told Hugh McIlvanney:

"With Ryan, in contrast, my advice was that he should always be trying to do the difficult things. If he does not make frequent attempts to do something apparently undoable, he is not being true to himself. There will be plenty of times when the effort fails, but when it succeeds, the best opposition the game can offer will be helpless. He took the breath away from Bobby Charlton and me when we first saw him a dozen years ago and he is capable of doing it every time he is at full surge. Of course, I am glad he has worked on acquiring a more rounded game but he must never forget how exceptional he is. Talking to him on Monday, I told him he was the forward that defenders in the Premiership least wanted to face because of what happened when he ran at them. I urged him to do that whenever he had a glimpse of an opportunity. How could anybody foresee what he did in the second half of extra-time? When he set off on that gallop, we were hanging on for dear life and hoping it would come down to penalties. It would be madness to say I even dreamt he could give us that ecstatic climax. All I did before the match was try to plant in Ryan's head the belief that he is entitled to be far more ambitious than 999 footballers out of a thousand. With his talent, he has an absolute right to attempt feats of extravagant brilliance on the field."

So it was that intercepting "a rather weary one from Vieira", Giggs ran with it instead, passing or somehow snaking between various challenges without ever quite appearing in control of the ball – or where he was going – until suddenly he was through on goal. "Pass it, for fuck's sake pass it, pass it" was hollered from the empty row just in front of the restricted view seats (and presumably by most Reds in the ground). Giggs, the world expert in ruining brilliant goals via the careless application of easy finishes, kept running, until suddenly the ball spat, roasted, hissed and burned into the roof of the net, and then it was all pubic chest hair, swinging shirts and pitch invasions.

"He just bobbed and weaved and kept going, and when he needed a finish, *my God* did he give us one", said Andy Gray. "The ultimate expression of the incredible natural gifts he has always had since he came to us as a 13-year-old" said Ferguson.

He's a funny one, Giggs. Partly because he was so good to begin with, partly because of injury, and partly just because of him, his career has never really peaked, and in United's greatest ever season he was the least effective of the first picks. If a player stays at any club for long enough, inevitably there'll be moments that are absolutely his, but now, Giggs had produced two within a week. Here was genuine brilliance from a man considered something of a flake by many: surely a more suitable testament to his talent than season-by-season evaluation.

For all their possession in extra-time, Arsenal couldn't muster much in the way of chances; Bergkamp forced Schmeichel into a flying save in the first period, and after our goal, Adams, all bohemian, lyre-playing hair, headed wide from a corner. Then it was all over, precipitating another pitch invasion.

After the game, Adams and Dixon visited the United changing room to offer congratulations: Rob Smyth later wrote in *The Guardian* that the teams "shared an unspoken mutual respect that might have been mistaken for homoeroticism in some cultures." Typically, Ferguson rose to the occasion too: naturally bullish, his interview in the tunnel was positively bodacious (look it up, it's worth it, I promise).

"This isn't what you need, really … you needed a result, but you didn't need extra time, 10 men, a real battle like this," Gary Newbon informed him.

"Look, who's to know what's gonnae happen in football, Gary" he replied. "It could all blow up in our face at the end of the day, but can you forget moments like this?"

A sheepish 'no' is faintly audible.

"Oor supporters will be talking about that for years, the players'll be talking about that for years, that's what football's about, trying to reach peaks and climaxes to a season, which we are doing at the moment. We're in a final, and we got something in the bank for ourselves, now we go and try and win this league."

That was the last FA Cup semi-final replay. Well done, football.

JUVENTUS AWAY, EUROPEAN CUP 21 APRIL 1999

That time you first beat your dad at tennis, or chess, or in a fight – it means something, and there's no going back. So, when United beat Juventus in October 1997, after improving each time from the first miserable effort in Turin a year earlier, and then went on to win every game until the group was won, they thought they might be there. But Juventus somehow skulked into the quarter-finals following a late Inzaghi goal in the return fixture, the second of two runners-up and ahead of Paris Saint-Germain on goal difference. They went on to appear in a third consecutive European Cup final, their fourth consecutive European final.

Typically, it was same again this time round. Going into the last round of group games, Rosenborg and Galatasaray had eight points, and Juve had five. To progress, they needed to beat Rosenborg at home – fair enough, they did – but they also needed Athletic Bilbao, owners of a measly three points, to win against Galatasaray – and they did. "Juventus have qualified?!" asked an incredulous Gary Neville after United's game with Bayern, his face falling so far as to require a team of geologists to extract it from the earth's core. They stab it with their steely knives, but they just can't kill the beast.

At half-time in the first leg, Fergie was confident that "if we can draw the game, then we'll always score", and he remained believably convinced before the second. "I feel good about it," he told ITV. "They'll come at us hundred mile an hour, they'll try to finish us off as they always do in the first thirty minutes…It's gonna be a great night, I hope."

And, of course, Juventus were confident too. "False modesty is not a Juventus trait," wrote *The Guardian's* Jim White on the morning of the game. "Indeed, after their magnificent performance at Old Trafford in the first leg, the air of certainty Juventus have already as good as qualified for their fourth Champions League final on the bounce is such that their coach, Carlo Ancelotti, has been trying to caution against complacency…'I told them they are not invincible.'"

Juve made two changes from the first leg, Brindelli in for the suspended Mirkovic, and Ferrara replaced Montero, who was deemed not to be match-fit. But most of the pre-match chatter surrounded Zinedine Zidane, whose Spanish wife wanted to go home. This incited owner, Gianni Agnelli, to tell the press that: "Zidane is suffering because he's under the thumb. I took him aside and asked: 'Who is the boss in your house – you or your wife?' He said since he'd had his two sons, his wife is. I'd love to have him at Juventus next season. The problem is the wife; I have no authority over her."

United lined up as expected. Giggs was unfit, so Blomqvist played wide on the left, Cole and Yorke returned after being rested for the previous two games, and Butt was preferred to Scholes in midfield – Fergie's only real selection dilemma for the big games.

"I don't think players ever see things from the manager's point of view, they look after themselves," said Butt. "I know I do. I am selfish about wanting to play every game. It's never nice to be told you are not in the team, but you've got to find a way of keeping your spirits up and staying fresh for the next one."

Though he never quite sustained the improvement he'd made in the autumn (most obviously evident in the home game against Leeds in which a belting winning goal almost obscured a dominant performance), it's arguable that he and not Scholes was the first-choice partner for Roy Keane. He was certainly preferred in many of the more important games, and participated in those that produced many of the team's finest performances. While Scholes's genius was obvious even then, he was a peripheral player too often to command automatic inclusion. Perhaps, coinciding with Keane's decline, his ability to properly conduct games came later and, with the exception of 1995-96 when he was deployed mainly as a striker, so did his most prolific seasons.

In Turin, the game began relatively slowly, United looking comfortable, until on four minutes, Zidane sent a diagonal ball right to left, to where Inzaghi had pilfered a half-yard from Stam. In the time it took him to control the pass, Stam reclaimed it, and averted the danger, but not for long. After Davids found Pesotto, Beckham conceded a corner, taken short by Zidane to Di Livio. While United's men on the posts vacated their positions – after all, who could have expected a corner-type cross, of all things, from a man in possession near the corner flag – everyone else did nothing, allowing Zidane to measure a ball to the back post, where, as Gary Neville later recalled, "Filippo Inzaghi nipped ahead and scored as I tried to rugby tackle him."

United came straight back; Keane, Yorke and Beckham exchanged passes, before Keane found Gary Neville. He lifted a cross into Cole, who made good contact on an overhead kick, but could only direct it at Peruzzi's pieholder, into which it was absorbed like so much before it. With United continuing to push the pace, the pattern of the game was set, all the more so when Pesotto fed Inzaghi on the left corner of the box, with his back to goal and to Stam. He feinted to turn inside, went outside, and with the split-second the subterfuge bought him, hit an early shot to turn what could have been a block into a deflection: 2-0.

"Manchester United need a minor miracle now," lamented the commentator, but that wasn't so; they'd played well enough in the opening 11 minutes to suggest that two unanswered goals were not beyond them. Peter Schmeichel recalled that after the Arsenal replay, "we felt unbeatable", and why wouldn't they? And they were. No flapping, shaking or sulking, just hard, fast skilful football taught by Matt Busby.

So a swift move between Beckham, Keane and Yorke ended with Cole given wrongly offside. Then, Blomqvist chested down, faced his own goal and swivelled into a reverse pass for the overlapping Irwin. His ball into Yorke was stepped over, lifted over the top by Cole, and collected with leaping chest control and a volley lashed just wide (a contribution good enough for Ron Atkinson to restore him to nickname terms following a brief demotion provoked by a poor piece of control).

You could feel it now, United were coming in the air tonight. Butt, joining things, bringing one sentence to an end and starting another, flicked on a Schmeichel punt and, suddenly, Yorke was in on goal. Ferrara, though, was not an Italian defender for no reason, taking a millisecond to pull on his shoulder, just enough to disturb his balance, before joining him on the grass. No foul said the referee.

On 24 minutes, Keane and Blomqvist exchanged passes to win a corner on the left, which Beckham curled into the near post. Rising early and rising alone, intense eyes clearly fixed on the ball, Keane willpowered in a glancing header, left Zidane on his anus, and ran back to get going again, without so much as a double-footed hop and arm flap.

The archetypal captain's goal was the defining moment of what would become his signature performance. He later said the fuss over it was "quite embarrassing actually," a typically contrarian sentiment but also an accurate one. Newcastle in December 1995, Liverpool in the 1996 Cup Final, Arsenal twice in 1999-2000, Madrid away in 2000, all immediately come to mind as superior efforts, but to identify specific games is almost to miss the point; it was the reliable brilliance, rather than its particular iterations, that was so astonishing.

And it was this that made him such an inspirational captain. Any moron can shout and bully, but like Robson and Cantona, the key to Keane's leadership was the knowledge that he would deliver in every single game. This ability was founded in an obsessive attention to significant detail, learnt from Brian Clough.

"If you weren't doing your stuff, Clough would spot it," he wrote in his autobiography. "A seemingly innocuous mistake that resulted in a goal conceded three or four minutes later, a tackle missed, or a failure to make the right run, or pass, would be correctly identified as the cause of the goal. It was no use pointing the finger at someone else – which is second nature to most players. He knew; you knew he knew. Every football match consists of a thousand little things which, added together, amount to the final score. The game is full of bluffers, banging on about 'rolling your sleeves up', 'having the right attitude' and 'taking some pride in the shirt'. Brian Clough dealt in facts, specific incidents, and invariably he got it right."

"Bluffer" is the ultimate insult in Keane's world; acting truthfully and according to principle are the only standards that must be satisfied. This refusal to compromise is psychologically demanding. Living in digs in Nottingham, he asked his landlady if he might decorate his room, and when she agreed, he painted the walls and ceiling black, claiming it was the only way that he could relax.

Lean, pinched and demonic, burning calories with the pure intensity of his being, he personified the red devil. "Aggression is what I do," he once said. "I go to war. You don't contest football matches in a reasonable state of mind." Opponents knew it, teammates knew it, and the crowd knew it; it's unlikely that any player has ever imposed his personality to such an over-whelming degree. In any place you called home, it'd be his word that found you.

After 28 minutes, possession statistics appeared on the screen: Juve 38, United 62. Cole held up the ball, prepared Yorke for a shot... he dragged it wide; it was all very weird: away to Juventus in a European Cup semi-final, and it's one-sided. Like the story of a man arriving at the scene of a road accident to find a person trapped under a car and, instinctively directing all his strength and adrenalin into the maelstrom of the moment, finding that he can lift it. That's what United were doing.

A minute later Juve almost scored again. Di Livio crossed from the left, Schmeichel attempted some sort of volleyball set, missed, and the ball hit Conte on the head. But as it looped goalwards, Stam raced after it in pursuit, slotted in behind and headed off the line like it was nothing.

Soon after, Blomqvist played an ill-advised square ball towards Butt, who let it go. But before it could reach Keane, Zidane nipped in to steal possession, and Keane brought him down with a lunge that was probably unnecessary. Booked and, accordingly, out of any potential final, he responded in typical fashion, distributing viscous chunks of his mind before carrying on as before.

Gary Neville was a man after his own black heart. "The way it was reported," he wrote, "Roy had been even more heroic following his booking – in contrast to Gazza crying at the 1990 World Cup in the same stadium – but I didn't see it that way. He'd done his job, outstandingly. Emotion hadn't come into it."

There followed a brief quiet period, before Neville – who had an exceptional evening – clipped one of his famous aimless passes around the corner. Only this time, Beckham leapt to nod it down towards Cole, whose first touch happened to prod it into an ideal crossing position. The cross was perfect, a pass almost, cutting out Ferrara – whose face flashed horror, followed by resignation – to where the Jumpman Yorke was waiting to do the rest.

"They have seen Juventus's away goal, and they have raised it!"

The tempo of Keane's passing did not permit United or Juve a moment's respite, ordering Irwin forward. His pass into Cole created the chance for a snap shot which he hit well; Peruzzi saved down to his right. Seconds later, a lofted ball from Di Livio bounced in such a way as to permit Inzaghi a shot. But as he waited for it to drop, Schmeichel was set, and consequently saved it easily.

Immediately, Neville and Beckham combined, Beckham slid a quick pass down the right for Cole. The ball travelled through Butt, Neville again and Keane, before the full-back hit a long pass towards Blomqvist. Ferrara headed clear, but Birindelli's error allowed Yorke to pick up possession 25 yards from goal. He floated clear of Iuliano, advanced, and flayed a low shot off the inside base of the far post. Blomqvist combined with Cole to initiate another stepover routine involving Yorke, but Iuliano intervened, and perhaps the finest half of football United have ever played – perhaps the finest half of football United will *ever* play – was over.

At full-time, Fergie would fully agree. At half-time, he only half-agreed. "We're playing great football," he said in the dressing room, before turning to the defence. "But you lot had better sort yourselves out."

Despite his admonishment, Juve created the first chance of the second period. Inzaghi took a pass from Di Livio and shot against Schmeichel, and so began a brief period of home supremacy. It ended with Yorke flicking on a Beckham cross, which Cole attempted to control when a shot would've served him better.

On 62 minutes, Stam headed a Di Livio cross clear, Blomqvist dithered on the ball, was robbed, and Conte shot, but Inzaghi, tapping in at the far post, was offside. That would be Blomqvist's final involvement, withdrawn for Scholes. He brought the usual calm authority to United's passing, involved in a move, along with Neville, Beckham and Yorke, that spanned the width of the pitch and ended with Irwin clicking a right-footed shot against the inside of the post, then a follow-up with his left into the side-netting.

Though they were trailing, Juve were unable to build momentum, with United always quick to move the ball forward. On 76 minutes, a frustrated Ferrara stuck his hand in Cole's face, Cole pursuing him to return a shove, then Scholes caught Deschamps and received a yellow card. He too would miss the final. "I didn't really make a bad tackle," he recalled, "but when I challenged him, he gave a bit of a scream, which some foreign players are liable to do, and I firmly believe that's what got me booked. I have to admit it came as a crushing blow, but there was never going to be any Gazza-type tears from me. You can get upset and disappointed, but it's only football and you have to keep perspective." Seconds later, he won the ball, stepped away from his man, and prompted an attack with an astute pass.

With 11 minutes remaining, United almost scored a third. Fonseca, brought on as Juve prepared to defend a corner, sliced off the line as Yorke was first to Beckham's cross. He then almost contributed at the other end, crossing for Amoruso, but Johnsen was alert and headed clear. He collected a reverse ball from Zidane on the left by-line, and his low cross was missed by Inzaghi. Stam allowed it through his legs, and away from goal.

That was as nervous as it got. United knitted together passes, one after another, but passes with purpose, and the move ended with a Cole shot. Juve tried another attack, and when that broke down Schmeichel punted a clearance downfield. Montero met it with a weak header, the ball dropped to Yorke, who inhaled deeply to wheedle through the tiny gap between him and Iuliano. As he rounded Peruzzi, the keeper pulled him down, but before the referee could award a penalty, Cole caught up with the loose ball and slipped it into the net.

"Full speed ahead Barcelona! Manchester United are in sight of the European Cup final again!"

That was pretty much it – although there was still time for Beckham to volley wide and call Davids 'a fucking wanker'. Juventus were the first Italian team in 20 years to lose a home knock-out tie in the European Cup; the final would not involve an Italian team for the first time in seven years. The word 'awesome' could legitimately be used, an event equally as infrequent. The Old Lady had been well and truly happy-slapped.

BAYERN MUNICH, EUROPEAN CUP FINAL 26 MAY 1999

*"Can Manchester United score? They always score... Peter Schmeichel is forward...Beckham, in towards Schmeichel, it's come for Dwight Yorke...cleared... Giggs with the shot...**Sheringhaaaaam!** ... Name on the trophy! Teddy Sheringham, with thirty seconds of added time played, has equalised for Manchester United, they are **still in the European Cup!***

*"You have to feel, this is their year. Is this their moment? Beckham into Sheringham...**and Solskjær has won it!** Manchester United have reached the promised land! Ole Solskjær! The two substitutes have scored the two goals in stoppage time, and the treble looms large.*

"History is made...Manchester United are the champions of Europe again. And nobody will ever win a European Cup final more dramatically than

this. Champions of Europe, champions of England, winners of the FA Cup, everything their hearts desired... Down and out, not a bit of it, they are never out. Memories are made of this forever and a day."

It was not just the most dramatic end to any football match that we'll ever see, or even the most dramatic end to a football match that anyone will ever see, but the single most dramatic event most of us will ever see in the course of our miserable lives. Grown men, staggering into collapses like drunks hit by lightning; bodies strewn everywhere, frozen at irregular angles; one lone man wailing, beating at the ground in shock, impotence, rage and despair. And all around them, tens of thousands of other men, celebrating joy like they couldn't believe.

There've been last-minute goals before. There've even been two last-minute goals before. But never in the last minute of the European Cup final, for a team trailing by one, and needing a win to complete an unprecedented treble.

Even still, it's not the success that's truly special, but the glory. The season featured every single facet that could possibly be desired of any season: astounding games, exceptional competition, manic determination, and shocking plot twists. Everything went right, and even when things went wrong they went right – because each of them contributed to the denouement. Sport makes the incredible credible; but even so, *this* was truly incredible. Yet it was credible because it happened. Or, to put it another way, it encompassed every *aspect* of a narrative that makes United, football, sport and life so compelling.

There's something within the psyche that drives us to seek out and tell stories, our own rarely as intriguing as those we adopt. Following a football team straddles those two aspects – us as extras in theirs, them a lead in ours. Our identity and life is bound up in the events, characters and experiences that surround United, the same as with any fan of any club – but no one else will ever have a season like that one, and no one else will ever have a team like that one.

A core of local kids mixed with expensive signings and unknowns; melding icons, greats and at least a couple of all-time greats. What more do you want? What more could you have?

Aggression, heart, beauty, intricacy, power, strength, imagination and testicles beyond compare. What more do you want? What more could you have?

A proper shade of red. What more do you want? What more could you have?

Aaaaahhhhhhh, Cantona, United in excelsis.

Has any team ever imagined as many memories? The last-minute eye bleeders; the heart-destroying moments; the endless perplexing variety of goals. If there was a shmicing to be dispensed, then dispensed a shmicing was, with extreme prejudice. In any normal, or even abnormal season, winning 6-2 twice and 8-1 once, all away from home, would be major events – yet in this one, they were almost incidental.

You have to wonder how it's possible to sustain an argument that this wasn't the finest British team of the modern era. In 55 years of trying, United are the first and only team to win league, Cup and European Cup in the same season, with the highest possible tariff of difficulty and the highest possible standard of execution. Given that we're here for our own gratification, let's gratify ourselves and spell it out.

United won arguably the best league in British football history. They finished above an excellent Chelsea side (which lost only three games), and an exceptional Arsenal one – one which had itself won the double the season before, boasted one of the finest defences in history, was tough, exciting and balanced, given an easy Cup run, and had no Europe with which to contend.

Conversely, aside from Fulham (runaway winners of the First Division), United beat a Premier League side in every round of the Cup, including Liverpool, Chelsea and Arsenal. To win the European Cup, they escaped a group containing Barcelona and Bayern Munich, then beat both the Italian sides in the competition – on aggregate, without the need for away goals – and then Bayern Munich, without resorting to extra time or penalties. That there were moments when it might have slipped away testifies to the quality of opposition and amplifies United's durability, brilliance under pressure, and aforementioned spermispheres.

They played fast, exciting, original football, regardless of the opposition or state of the game. Famous for late goals, they scored just as many early, and required no elaborate tactics: defend properly, attack whenever possible, enjoy.

So what to do afterwards? Should any team complete a subsequent treble... well, it's been done by United already, in circumstances that we can be confident are superior. Yet, the paradox is that this applies to United too, a double paradox the knowledge that were it not for affluence already encountered, we'd be content to remain impoverished in the future.

But let's not finish with existential crisis. As Fergie later wrote, "the celebrations begun by that goal will never really stop. Just thinking about it can put me in party mood", and he's right. We're obligated to savour it, to savour it every day of our lives, because that's as good as it's gonna get and it won't get that good again.

Daniel Harris is a writer - on football, mainly for The Guardian - and author of United book On The Road, a journey through a season - @danielharris. He was shortlisted for best best new writer at the 2011 British Sports Book Awards.

ACKNOWLEDGEMENTS

Working as editor on a book about the team you've supported since the year dot would be most football supporters' defintion of a dream job. I'm no different. Heading into the office to put together a Manchester United anthology is a pretty good way to spend your working day.

The writers, journalists and bloggers who contributed to *Deepest Red* have been unstinting in their enthusiam for the project. Their work captures brilliantly the spirit of Manchester United and for that I thank them.

All were extremely helpful, but special mention must go to Daniel Harris who provided much needed advice and feedback throughout *Deepest Red's* gestation.

Special thanks also to the team at Portnoy Publishing for their hard work and assistance over the course of this project (including the Arsenal supporters!).

Brian Foley
November 2012

Portnoy

PUBLISHING